THE ART OF BEING A SINGLE WOMAN

By the same author:
    Someone There: Making Sense of Christianity (SCM)
    Drawing Near To The City (SPCK)
    Lent for Busy People (BRF)
    Married To The Church (SPCK)
    My World (BRF)

The Art of Being a Single Woman

SHELAGH BROWN

KINGSWAY PUBLICATIONS
EASTBOURNE

Copyright © Shelagh Brown 1989

First published 1989

Unless otherwise stated biblical quotations are from the
Revised Standard Version copyrighted 1946, 1952
© 1971, 1973 by the Division of Christian Education of
the National Council of the Churches of Christ in the USA

Front cover photo: Zefa Picture Library

British Cataloguing in Publication Data

Brown, Shelagh
    The art of being a single woman.
    1. Single women. Christian life
    I. Title
    248.8'43'2

ISBN 0-86065-584-9

Production and printing in Great Britain for
KINGSWAY PUBLICATIONS LTD
1 St Anne's Road, Eastbourne, E Sussex BN21 3UN by
Nuprint Ltd, 30b Station Road, Harpenden, Herts AL5 4SE

Contents

I

The Art of Being a Single Woman

'It's lovely to see you,' said the man whose party it was, putting his arms round me and giving me a large hug and an enthusiastic kiss. 'I can't think why you've never married! It's such a waste!' He said it the minute he greeted me, and I felt like shaking him. A waste of what?

But I knew what he meant, because it wasn't the first time he'd said it—and when I had tried to talk about it he wouldn't be serious. He would just look at me, smiling and appreciative, with a twinkle in his eye and not really listening to what I said. He knew what his opinion was, and nobody was going to change it. It was a waste that any attractive woman wasn't fulfilling her real purpose in life, which was to be someone's wife.

But little boys don't grow up believing that their real purpose in life is to be someone's husband. They daydream about being an astronaut or a pop star or a physicist or a high-powered businessman or a mountaineer or a footballer. Whatever the dream happens to be at the time it is always about what they are going to *do*.

There could well be a woman somewhere in the dream doing what their mother currently does for them: comforting and loving and cleaning and feeding. But she won't be at the centre of the dream. She will be somewhere out on the edges. What really interests them is what they are going to achieve, and when their dream comes true they are going to be a hero or a Superman.

But these days stories are not just about Superman. Nowadays Superwoman whirls herself round on the television screen and does incredible and impossible things. A few years ago Shirley Conran wrote a book entitled *Superwoman*[1] telling us how to be a working wife and mother, a housemaid, a laundrymaid, a superb decorator, a brilliant organiser and (for good measure) how to cope with sexual aggression if we were single. It was almost as incredible and impossible as Superwoman on the screen, but it was fascinating and useful and practical, and the moment I got home with it I read it from cover to cover. When I had finished I realised that a married woman (with or without children) who did a job was also expected to fulfil all the other traditional roles *as well*, and to do them enormously successfully. But the problems that those expectations confront women with are not for dealing with here.

What this book is really about is how those of us who are single women can be fulfilled human beings. I have called it *The Art of being a Single Woman* because an art is a skill that we acquire through knowledge and practice. Then, when we have made it our own, we use it to make a work of art.

A lovely translation of Ephesians 2:10 in the New Jerusalem Bible says that 'We are God's work of art, created in Christ Jesus for the good works which God has already designated to make up our way of life.' You are God's work of art, and so am I – and to get it right we have to work at it as well as God.

Paul told the Christians in Philippi to 'work out your own salvation with fear and trembling, for it is God who is at work within you both to will and to do of his good pleasure' (Phil 2:12–13). We have to collaborate with God so as to fulfill the possibilities that God has already put within us, what he 'has already designated . . .'. To designate is 'to destine to a purpose'. So you are called to fulfill your destiny, and I am called to fulfill mine.

But what is our destiny? What sort of woman does God want you to be—and me to be? The winds of change are blowing, and women are dreaming dreams. Sometimes they are the wrong dreams. But we are in the process of waking up, like Sleeping Beauty in her prison of thorns—kissed into wakefulness by the Spirit of God. The promise given a long time ago was that the Spirit would be poured out on men *and* on women, and when that happened we would be set free from the old ways that went back to the banishment from Eden. God said to the woman: 'Your yearning will be for your husband, and he will dominate you' (Gen 3:16).

Those words describe how it has been for thousands of years, and we have only rarely found the freedom that the prophets prophesied about and the gospel promised.

'Love is to man a thing apart, 'tis woman's whole existence', and there is that in a woman's heart which can feel that our whole existence and well-being is dependent on the love of a man. We can be like ivy, clinging round a tree and taking our life from it by thousands of little roots. Poor tree! Struggling to survive with this parasite living off it. Poor women, because we are meant to be rooted and grounded in the love of God—not taking our life and our meaning from a man.

There are several reasons why I am not married, and you will probably find out most of them in the course of this book. One reason was that I felt that I had to find my own identity *apart from a man* before I could marry one. Otherwise I would have got my status and my value and my meaning from my husband, and those things would all have been contingent to him.

Another reason was that I wanted to go on my own adventure of living. When I had endlessly read fairy stories as a small girl it was nearly always the youngest son in a family who went off and did brave deeds, and when he had done them successfully he usually got a princess as a prize. I never noticed it at the time, but on the whole princesses were astonishingly passive, and never made even a squeak of complaint when their father handed them over to the most successful applicant.

The next type of literature I moved on to had a different model, and in the schoolgirl stories that I used to love to read the heroine was successful and popular and a winner as a person in her own right.

But when I left behind schoolgirl stories and started to read love stories they went back to something much nearer the fairy-tale model. The heroine was 'successful' when she met the man of her dreams, and after various predictable hiccups in the relationship she was carried off, passive and delighted, into the 'great white bridal bed' which is the inevitable ending to a Barbara Cartland novel. In the bridal bed there was consummation, union, entire satisfaction and total bliss, and that was where the story ended.

In many ways that was just what I longed for. But my true self, deep down in the heart of me, couldn't tolerate it and rejected it passionately, because that self wanted to be rooted and grounded in God. However long it took (and so far it's been half a lifetime since I set out on the quest) I had to get my union and communion with God right before I could manage that union and communion with a man which marriage seemed to be about.

Recently, I discovered that a Roman Catholic priest called Sebastian Moore had put my struggle into words in *The Inner Loneliness*, and as I recognised it I found myself saying with great delight and excitement 'Yes, *that's* it!'

Sebastian Moore writes of the age-old split between man and woman, and says that it is a loneliness that only God can heal. It is only 'in the mind of God that man and woman are one; but our inner loneliness yearns to be touched by that mind . . . Everything radical in the human, his/her sexuality, his/her earth dependence, his/her morality, *is* that loneliness in search of its unimaginable friend.'

Once we become aware of this, he says, we can become aware of something that we might otherwise miss in the creation story in Genesis, although it is in fact very obvious:

> It is the story of man and woman and God. It is the emotional story of man and woman and God. God creates first not a man (*ish*) but an human (*Atham*— Adam), sees it is lonely and splits it into man (*ish*) and woman (*isha*).

> The meaning is, that they will find their meaning in each other but only provided they find the meaning of their respective 'halving' of the human whole in God. . . .

> To the man who is finding God within himself, the woman is not just a mysterious other-half but a person anchored in the eternal. And the same applies of course to the vision of him that she is to have. . . .[2]

In *The Power of Love* Bishop Fulton Sheen wrote that 'No man is the final goal of any woman, nor is any woman the ultimate purpose of any man. God is the end of both.'[3] When we have allowed that truth to sink deeply into our minds and become part of us we shall experience a new freedom and happiness. It is a truth that married women need to know just as much as single women.

Paul wrote to the Christians in Rome telling them, 'Do not be conformed to this world but be transformed by the renewal of your mind, that you may prove what is the will of God, what is good and acceptable and perfect' (Rom 12:2). The way of our own transformation will be to keep affirming the truth and denying what is false. We need to put some new software in the computer and start listening to the truth going on inside our heads.

'In Christ . . . there is neither male nor female . . .' (Gal 3:26,28). That doesn't mean that we are unisex. It means that the old divisions between us have gone—like the wall in the Temple at Jerusalem that kept women in their court, out of the Temple itself.

We are each a member of the Christian family, the sons and daughters of God. So if we give to God his title of 'King of Kings and Lord of Lords', that makes every woman who is a daughter of God into a princess. That gives us a new status, and once we really get the fact of it into our heads it will set us free from all our feelings of inferiority (because feelings always follow from facts: never the other way round).

In *Nightfall*, a Lion paperback by Christopher Bryan, Charlie Brown has called the woman he loves princess, and she writes him a letter: 'Charlie Brown, I have loved you. That's a fact. And nothing can alter it. I have loved you. Weeks ago (centuries it seems) when we first met, I remember writing in my diary, 'Today Charlie called me princess.' You didn't just call me princess. You made me feel like one. Thank you. Jacquie.'[4]

But even without a Charlie Brown in our lives to call us princess it is still possible to know that we are. The knowledge and the certainty and the glory of it will come direct from the King of Kings who is our Father.

This book is a practical book. Since it is about learning the art of being a single woman it includes practical things like buying a home, running a car, having people to meals, going to work and going on holidays. It is also about the theology behind all those things. Theology is not a dry, academic discipline. It is that study which deals with God, his nature and attributes, and his relations with man (or men and women, because the word *man* means the whole human race) and the universe. It includes everything that there is in the universe, because God has made everything that there is. Theology is a means through which we encounter God and through which God encounters us. What does God say to us through our home, through our car, and through the clothes that we wear? What does God say to us through the meals that we eat and through the work that we do, or through the holidays that we take (or fail to take)? What do we say to God about them?

So theology (and therefore this book as well) is also about the practice of prayer: because prayer is the conversation between God and men and women as well as being the means through which we experience and enjoy that relationship.

Finally, I have talked with other Christian women about the art of being single. I had originally planned to incorporate what they said in what I wrote (though of course telling you who had said what). But they said such good and profound things that I wanted to include everything. So that is what I have done—and if you read this book in order you will read them next. My own chapters come afterwards.

Mother Frances Dominica is the founder of Helen House in Oxford. Ruth Etchells was until recently the Principal of St John's College, Durham. She is also a writer. Dr Ruth Fowke is a psychiatrist and a writer. The Revd Patsy Kettle is a Deacon. She recently married at the age of forty plus, but that does not disqualify her from speaking about the single life, since she had a long experience of it. Dr Helen King works in academic research and is a member of the General Synod. Aredi Pitsiaeli is a conference organiser and personal assistant to Pete Meadows of Spring Harvest. Rosemary Stevens is a librarian in the University of London. Doreen Ayling is the personal assistant to Ruth Etchells and a widow. Joyce Blackwell is a head teacher in a primary school and leads Highway Holiday Houseparties on the continent. She is also a widow. I thought it was important to include the views of women who have had the experience of widowhood, because learning the art of being single again after being married comes in a special category and can be especially painful.

I hope that you will find what we all have to say both interesting and helpful, and that because of it you will be even better at practising the art of being single—to the greater glory of God.

Aredi Pitsiaeli

Aredi Pitsiaeli is the conference manager for Bridgehead Communications and personal assistant to Peter Meadows. She has worked for him for eight years and was his assistant during the Luis Palau Mission to London when he was the Director. She trained as a secretary at the BBC and worked for the Managing Director of BBC Radio for two years. Her family consists of her mother (whom she lives with), two brothers (Yannakis, who is married, and Andreas) and dog Nicky. Aredi likes acting, singing, reading, playing tennis, listening to music, spending time with her family and her friends, and going out to the theatre, the cinema and for meals. When our interview was finished we went out for a delicious Greek meal in a nearby restaurant, where the Greek proprietor welcomed Aredi like a member of his family and made a delightful fuss of us.

Aredi is attractive and still within the normal age range for getting married. So I started off our interview by asking her why she wasn't. She said, 'That's a question I keep asking myself! Why? I really don't know. I've had opportunities. My father was Greek, and most Greek girls are married in their late teens or early twenties. My cousin married when she was eighteen. When I was eighteen it was usual that people had their marriages arranged—even in England. I don't know that it happens quite so much now. I think it's beginning to die out.

'So when I got to the age of eighteen they said, "We'll introduce you to these nice Greek boys. . . .!" And they produced quite a few "nice Greek boys". If I had let it go further it could have done. There were two of them who would have liked that.

'But at that point I had become a Christian and because of that, and also because I was a person who rebelled against that kind of arranged marriage, I just didn't want it. It wasn't going to be for me, and it caused enormous problems with my father and huge arguments and ructions in the family. But I said "At this stage of my life this sort of marriage is not what I want".'

It was at this time that Aredi joined the local Baptist church. But she didn't meet anybody through the youth group. 'I did meet a few people through my work,' she told me, 'but nothing really jelled. I don't know why. There is no reason that I can think of and I went through the whole gamut of reasons: "There must be something terribly wrong with me." "I'm ugly!", or "I'm fat" or "I've got a big nose" I would think there must be some physical reason. There must be something strange about me.

'Then a woman told me, "You're too strong a person. You put the men off".' That was the sort of silly comment I would expect from a boy, but it was from a woman, and it really shocked me. So I thought, "Well, maybe that's it. Maybe I am too strong a personality." So I spent time trying to quieten my personality. But then I thought, "This is absolutely ridiculous, I'm not that sort of person: I'm me, and if people don't like me the way I am then that's just tough".'

It was tough, and Aredi went through some times of feeling very depressed, when she wondered, 'Why me?'. And it probably became harder because she says 'I had been brought up to believe that this was the natural progression. This was what was going to come next. Like most of us, I assumed I was going to be married, and there was absolutely no doubt in my mind that I would be. I never thought there might be another path for me.'

For Aredi, like others of us, it wasn't really until her mid-twenties that she started to say to herself: 'Hold on a minute! I think I'm doing all the right things, but nothing's really happening. Maybe I've got to rethink my whole view of marriage and children. It was only then that I started to realise that perhaps it wasn't a forgone conclusion that I would have my husband and two children.'

That was a huge struggle and it still is. 'I go through peaks and troughs,' she told me, 'and I have times of being very down. I was basing my whole life on this fairy tale idea that a knight in shining armour was going to come along and carry me off into wonderland, and it really is hard to come to terms with the fact that it probably won't happen like that and that marriage may not be for me. It has been an enormous struggle and it is one that I am still going through, although I think I am beginning to sort out some of the issues.'

I asked her what the issues were, and she said: 'Well, first of all you feel that if you are not going to be married you are going to be very lonely. Because you will get older, and you won't have your family and your parents any more to be close to you and to love you. So I feel that. I won't have anybody. And I get in an utter panic.

'The other side of it is that I shan't have children. I shan't have people to come after me who are part of me. I suppose the way I am beginning to try and get sorted out is to realise that if I make good friendships and have close friends then part of that loneliness can go. That is something I am beginning to find, because I have got some very good friends. They are nice people to have around and they are supportive. They make me feel loved and valued and wanted.

'But I don't feel that will always be sufficient, because a husband and children are something very special, and it isn't going to be exactly the same just to have good friends. That is something you've just got to face.'

But Aredi was well aware that married people have their problems too. 'It must be awful to be disappointed with your partner,' she said shrewdly. 'If you have a

starry eyed view of marriage and what a husband ought
to be, it must be enormously disillusioning to find out
that this person is just as human as you are. He's going
to let you down, and then you're going to have all the
feelings of hurt and perhaps rejection—as well as the
good side of the marriage. I am sure there are pros and
cons to it, which I didn't think at one stage. I used to
think "It's just awful being single. It must be wonderful
to be married." I have had to begin to learn that isn't
always the case.

'Sometimes when I'm spending an afternoon with my
married friends and their children are with us all the
time I suddenly feel absolutely exhausted, and I think
"I'm just not used to this at all—what a tie they are!" If
I want to go out somewhere I can just go.

'But it doesn't take away the yearning if someone
wants to be married. You just begin to see things a bit
more clearly and a bit more logically.'

I asked Aredi if she would ever marry a non-Christian,
and she gave me a very honest answer. 'I'd like to say
"no" and I'm ninety-nine per cent sure that it is "no".
But I don't think you can ever be totally sure. You've
only got to meet someone who perhaps you've got very
similar interests to—and your emotions perhaps will
start running away with you. Who knows. I hope I can
say I have a strong enough faith. But speaking honestly I
wouldn't like to say one hundred per cent. I hope I
wouldn't, because I think I would miss out on a lot. And
in the end it would have to matter.'

I wondered if Aredi's Christianity helped her in her
situation as a single woman. 'It does and it doesn't. In
some ways it complicates things, because it can seem
that being single is a punishment. I must have done
something wrong to be left in the single state, because
God has missed me out. This has made me rethink my
whole view of God. I thought "Well, if God's this loving
God who really cares for me (and I believe that) this

must be what's right for me." Yet it just seemed so wrong. It seemed so wrong that I was on my own and that I wasn't going to have a family. So in some ways it has been hard, because being single has challenged my faith.

'I have been in a situation where I have thought that either what I believe about God is wrong, or if it's right then this must be the best for me. And that's hard to cope with.

'But then there is the positive side that knowing God and having a relationship with him does make it easier. I'm not quite sure how. Sometimes it's not very tangible. But perhaps when I'm feeling very down or very lonely and then I've prayed I've often felt a sense of peace. Not always. Sometimes I've just gone on feeling extremely down! But there can be this feeling that I am not absolutely alone—not totally—and then I don't feel that I am just struggling away on my own. There are times when I have felt "There is a purpose in all of this . . ."'.

I wondered if Aredi prayed about it when she was feeling depressed and lonely. 'It depends how down I am,' she said. 'If I am extremely down then often I can't. I know those are the very times when you should actually bring all your problems to God, but you can be so down that you can't see the wood for the trees. You just think, "I can't cope with this. It's just awful."

'Then there's a side of you that starts to feel a bit rebellious towards God and you say, "I won't talk to you! You're being horrible to me!" If perhaps there is someone that I quite like and it isn't working out then I think, "Oh God, why can't it work out? Why? I'd just rather not get involved at all—Why don't you stop it happening?" I know that sounds a bit stupid, because you're bound to keep meeting people. But then when you start to get hurt it's hard to understand why God doesn't protect you from it.'

I asked Aredi what she found the advantages and the

plusses to not being married, and she said 'Well, I really do appreciate having my own time to myself. Some of my friends are always having to think about being with their children and nappies and things like that. I don't have to worry about stopping in and I don't have to consider a husband. I think that's a big plus—even though I'd like a nice husband!

'Also, because I've got time, I can do things. I can get involved in activities that I wouldn't be able to get involved in if I was married and had children. I have been involved in all sorts of church activities as well as things outside the church. I was YPF leader for quite a few years and I spent a lot of time dealing with young people.

'I was Worship Group Leader, and I found that quite demanding. But it felt quite strange, and I am sure that because I am a woman I was treated differently than if I'd been a man. There were a few people who couldn't quite cope with a woman standing up and leading worship. They found it difficult, although there were others who appreciated it.

'I was the leader of the group and we used to take part in every Sunday service, with me introducing the songs and leading the worship, for most of the services. Nobody ever came up to me or wrote me a horrible letter, although one person said in a group discussion, "I don't think women ought to lead worship" and I took that fairly personally! But it was in little ways that they treated me differently. For instance, I would give my opinion on something and I'd say, "Well, could we do it this way?" And often they would listen to what I had to say, but there were other times when I felt they were almost patting me on the head, and they wouldn't have done that to a man. I know they wouldn't. Yet because I was a woman it was a case of, "Yes, all right, there there, dear".'

I thought Aredi would probably agree that women are

not as valued as they should be in leadership roles in the church. 'Yes. It's fine if you want to help with Sunday school or if you want to do the church cleaning. You can do that. But if you get to a position of authority there are still people who can't cope with it. They don't think it's right.

'I know the contribution I made really did help a lot of people. It's very difficult, because I don't want to be antagonistic, but at the same time why shouldn't I use the gifts God has given me? I always felt there was a bit of a fight. I had to speak louder than anyone else if I was going to get across what I felt was right.'

'Do you think that puts an additional burden on a single woman?' I asked her.

'Yes, I do. Perhaps it is because you feel vulnerable anyway when you're single, then since you are a woman as well, and you are having to fight because of that, it's a double burden.

'It is as if you are fighting with age-old prejudices, like the view that really a woman's worth is in her husband. And it is a tough struggle. But even when you are having to fight you still don't want to lose your femininity, and if you have got to shout louder than anybody else you feel as if you are turning into a strident feminist, which you don't want to be. Yet in order to get your views across you sometimes have to be a bit like that, and I don't want to be.

'But I'm fed up with the frustration of always being seen as the baby sitter and I am fed up with the way some people treat me because I'm single.'

Aredi, like many others of us who are single (men as well as women), has experienced the gross insensitivity and impertinence of people who ought to know better. We all have stories to tell of such behaviour. Here are two of Aredi's.

'I came out of church one day with a young man who's probably the last person on earth that I would ever want to marry (and I expect he feels just the same way about me), and the minister said to both of us (and I can't quote him exactly, but this is the gist of it. . . .) "We haven't had many weddings recently. How about you two getting together?" He actually said that. I thought "I can't believe it! How embarrassing." The guy was embarrassed and made some stupid comment, and I was embarrassed and just said, "I don't think so." I tried to make light of it.

'Then another day a very well meaning old lady came up to me in church, there having been a wedding the previous Saturday. She said, "Oh, your turn next!" I was standing there with a whole group of people, and I made some stupid comment like "Oh, I shouldn't think so," which made me feel I was worth nothing because to get myself out of the embarrassment I had to put myself down and make a joke of it.'

There was one final thing that had to be talked about that for Aredi and for many single people is an immense struggle: the physical side of not being married. Aredi said, 'Sometimes I feel I simply can't bear it, and when it's like that the only thing I can do is to accept that that's the way I feel. God made sex, and it's quite normal. So there's nothing wrong with feeling like I do. But those times are very hard. I have to be aware that for me there are certain times in the month when that feeling becomes stronger, and you simply have to accept that it is going to be very strong then. It's not easy.

'But then life isn't easy, is it? Whatever state you are in there is some struggle that you have to go through.'

Ruth Etchells

I first encountered Ruth Etchells twenty years ago through a book she wrote: *Unafraid to be: A Christian study of contemporary English writing*. It asked and answered the profoundest questions of the human heart: What is man? Who am I? What gives me identity? Contemporary secular writers were suggesting that our individual identity lies in the work we do, the values we hold and the relationships we enter into. Ruth showed that Christians also find their identity and understand a meaning in life as a whole through a relationship. But this is not an unstable experience, at the mercy of our changing feelings and affections. It is the sure relationship between us and God.

That book was a highlight for me. But I didn't meet Ruth in person until she gave a lecture to those of us who were doing post-ordination training in the Diocese of Southwark. The lecture was as brilliant as her book—and she told us of the extraordinarily moving Christ-figure of Matty in William Golding's *Darkness Visible*. So I bought that book, and found myself discovering more of what love is like and what it can do for another person.

Ruth always makes me think, and think more clearly, about God, Christ and ourselves—and she does it by reflecting theologically on the ordinary things of life. You will discover how she does it when you are reading about her cats, looking out through a balcony at the river in Durham.

Until the summer of 1988 Ruth Etchells was the Principal of St John's College, Durham, but she has just taken early retirement. St John's is a tall building in one of those beautiful, narrow, winding Durham streets. I have interviewed Ruth there on another occasion, but we actually conducted this interview on the telephone.

We had both been exceedingly busy, so we began with a general conversation about how we were, and I said that I had simply been sitting on my sofa reading a detective story and getting away from it all with my phone turned off. Typically with Ruth, this conversation immediately moved into deeper levels about our vital need for time to ourselves, so I said, 'Wait! Please don't say any more about that! I'd like to include it in the interview!'

So she waited until I had turned on the right switches on my machine, and then went on. 'I find that I cannot exist now,' she told me, 'unless I can manage to find a calm space somewhere. We seem to have lost our sense that there is as much godwardness in taking time to be quiet as there is in being busy with good works. Sometimes I turn the telephone off and just lie on the couch and look at the sky, and my animals climb all over me.

'They very much approve of it and they have taught me a lot about God. They teach me about dependency. I actually got my first dog when my mother was dying, because I suddenly realised that I would have nobody to think about but me. So I decided that what I must do was to get a little creature whose needs I would have to attend to.

'I have seen how selfish people can become who live alone and have no creature to consider but themselves, and it seemed to me that if I laid this upon myself before Mother died then it would be something that I really would have to go on with—even when I knew what a tide of misery would be sweeping over me. I think that has been very good for me, because however sad times have been, and however jubilant, there has always been this steady necessity to go on making sure that the animals are fed and watered and I am giving time and affection to them.

'Then I have found myself marvelling more and more at their innocence. They give one a glimpse of the real nature of innocence. It is something to do with a lack of self-consciousness and just a liking of life. One of the lovely things in my life is to watch my dog out for her walk—every muscle quivering with pleasure at the sheer joy of it.

'Another thing I love to do is simply to watch my cats out on the balcony. They stand with their heads between the railings and they are sniffing the riverbank below—every bit of them at full stretch. They are full of the morning and what the day is going to give them—and they are just lovely. They aren't doing all that because I am watching them. They are just doing it.

'A friend once said to me, when I was watching my cat, that he thought one of the finest advertisements for natural theology was a cat washing herself. I think he meant that its beauty and its orderliness—the way its function and its beauty went together—said something about the nature of creation.'

I asked Ruth whether she felt that the single life was in any sense an inferior life, and her answer was that it wasn't necessarily so, but that it had to be worked at tremendously hard in order not to be. So I asked her to tell me in what areas it was likely to be inferior. She said, 'The great danger in singleness is that you don't exercise your faculty of loving enough. Because the endless demands of a family are not being made you can much more easily live just to yourself. If you do that then it is an inferior life.

'In my twenties and thirties my battles and problems were about wanting someone to love me. But for the last twenty years that has seemed far less of a problem to me than not loving. Even now I really have to keep an eye on how selfish I can get, simply because once my last family contact had died there was no one there to make insistent demands on me. So I think the single life *can* be inferior, because it doesn't put one in a situation where there is always someone there who has to be loved. Yet once you are aware of it then there is far more space to love more widely. You have more time and freedom to give generously all over the place. So it doesn't need to be an inferior life at all. But we have got to be very aware of the dangers.

'The church has sometimes seen the celibate life as a superior life. But I believe it is a rare calling, and it is not how God has created us to be. He is a good and loving creator, who has created us in that form in which we were intended to live most fully. Therefore I cannot believe that his highest calling is for us to reject the way he made us. So I do not agree with the church when it has said that.

'Yet I believe that single people who have chosen virginity rather than promiscuity, because life has not given them a partner, are saying something very important in our society, especially in view of some of the things that are being said these days about lesbianism and homosexuality. People seem to think that if you happen to be lesbian or homosexual it is a quite appalling deprivation if you cannot fulfil your sexual instincts, and that this denial is something which should not be expected of you. But it seems to me that it is no different for those whose circumstances have made them single but who wouldn't have chosen to be single. The same richnesses are available to lesbian and homosexual single people as there are to single people who are heterosexual.

'In his *Diary of Prayer* John Bailey speaks of asking God every day how to use every disappointment as material for hope, and every pain as material for serenity.

'If we have experienced the distresses and lonelinesses that come from involuntary singleness, and then give those to God, our calling is somehow or another to work with him so as to use that material for the very opposite of loneliness—which is about openness to people and, even deeper than that, about openness to God.

'When I discovered God and realised that I had been found by him the most important thing for me was not anything to do with the forgiveness of sins. It was simply the astonishing realisation that God loved me. It was only years later that the whole issue of the forgiveness of sins became important. The first thing that happened for me that mattered was to know that I was loved.

'If those of us who are single can discover the extraordinary reality of the truth that God loves us then this is the basis for transforming the extraordinary pain of human loneliness. It transforms it by using it as material for a deeper understanding of what the loving of God is about. It isn't an easy transformation, but it is immensely important.'

I asked Ruth how any of us who don't feel loved could change that. How could someone set about knowing the love of God (towards them—it is what is known as a subjective genitive) shed abroad in their hearts?

'I think there are two paths to this,' Ruth answered. 'One is to know the truly Christian loving of a friend—a love that is really Christlike and wants God for them. In that sort of loving you get a faint mirror-image of the love of God, and I believe we often need some sort of human channelling of God's love.

'That is why there is such a need for us really to love people for God's sake: not because we are attracted to them, but for God's sake. It seems to me that a Christian loving friendship is different from any other kind of relationship, and I am not sure that there is enough of it in the church. If people don't feel themselves loved by God then the Christians around them are probably failing in really loving them.

'So that is the first way. The second way that I discovered the love of God was primarily through Scripture. It was by dwelling on the shatteringly powerful expression of the love of God in the first letter of John, and then meditating on what the incarnation actually was—and realising that it was about me. When those two things come together there could not be a more powerful statement that God loves me.'

'Can I just pick you up on one point?' I asked her. 'You said that we are to love other people not because we are attracted to them but for God's sake. I dare say some people do love me like that, and that they do it so beautifully that I haven't noticed—but I don't think it is how I want to be loved. I want to be loved just because I'm me—not because someone thinks they *ought* to love me and is just doing it for God's sake!'

'No! Any element of do-gooding is absolutely useless,' Ruth said. 'But Jesus never did that. Really loving for God is being aware of somebody, and immensely delighting in them because this is God's person—and you can't stop revelling in what it is that God is savouring in them. That's what I mean by it. It has nothing to do with compassion or with improving them or doing my duty by them. It's just creation. It's rather like the animals— delighting in this being simply because this being is of God.'

'Yes,' I said. 'I know what you mean, because I virtually never "don't like people", if that's not a too complicated negative. It's about seeing them as unique and rather marvellous. Yes, they can be very awkward—but when I actually attend to them I think they are all enchanting. But then sometimes I'll come up against a horrible priest who hates women, and then I'll start hating back and I don't see anything unique or marvellous at all!'

'Yes, that's the real crunch, isn't it?' Ruth said sympathetically. 'I bump into them sometimes, and trying to concentrate hard on what in them God is delighting in is a very difficult discipline. But I find that when I am very angry with a man who has handled me in this "priestly" way, and I am seething and hurt and very bruised, then one of the very few things that helps to allay that or soothe it a bit is actually to try to see what God must see in them. Although it doesn't take away the hurt it somehow takes away a bit of the anger.'

Rosemary Stevens

Rosemary Stevens works in one of the libraries of the University of London. She looks after the journals with the help of three assistants, whom it is her job to train. She was a member of Westminster Chapel, London, during the last ten years of Dr Lloyd-Jones's ministry. Two years ago she moved from a flat into a small house, which she is buying on a mortgage. She learned to drive in her forties, and now has a car. She likes being outdoors, nature, gardening, books, and conversations with her friends.

Since Rosemary moved to her house she has become the delighted owner of two cats, who give her great pleasure but a certain heartache. In a recent letter to me she wrote 'Talk about nature! On this perfect summer evening, I was sitting peacably in the garden when over the fence comes Hodge with a frog in his mouth, which had to be rescued by me!'

Rosemary and I have known each other for a long time, and I knew she had greatly valued Dr Lloyd-Jones's ministry. So I asked her to tell me what it had meant to her.

'I was brought up in a Christian home,' she said, 'and I had always been brought up on the Bible. But when I went to Westminster Chapel I realised that in fact I knew very little about what the Bible teaches us, in any systematic way.

'I remember the first time I went to the Chapel for the Friday evening Bible study. For the first time in my life I heard about the great doctrine of justification by faith from Romans 4 and what it means to the Christian. What the Doctor said was so easy to take in, and so interesting and stimulating, that you hardly realised how much you were being taught. You were taught how to think from the Bible for yourself, and how to find out what it was teaching and how to approach it. You don't dive straight into a problem. You set yourself back from it and then put it in its context of the whole teaching of the Bible about life in this world and why things are as they are.'

I asked Rosemary what sort of people went to the Chapel. Were they mostly married or single?

'There were families who formed the backbone. The men who became deacons, and their wives. Then there were heaps of young people who were passing through London. They were away from home, and just came together there because they wanted to hear that preaching and profit by being under that sort of ministry while they were in London, which was usually only for three or four years.

'The people I got to know were mostly like myself—working in London and away from home. When I started going to the Sunday afternoon Bible class I got to know people and we did things on Saturdays and went on holiday together.

I wondered if Rosemary felt that as a single woman she was as valuable in the church as married people were.

'It was back in the sixties,' she said, 'before the days of the consciousness raising of women. There was very little awareness in my generation that you should feel any kind of consciousness of yourself and your status. I was so busy enjoying the Christian friends I was making and learning so much that the actual structure of the church was irrelevant to me. The church was there, and other people were seeing to all the things that went on. There were heaps of people like me at that time. Youngsters. It was quite different to how I might feel today.'

So I asked her how she did feel today in her present church and whether she was perfectly happy.

'I feel rather a spectator,' she told me. 'But I don't think I've got it totally sorted out yet as a woman. I think women have different things to do according to the position they have been given in life. If you are in charge of a family that is very different from being a single woman whose energies are directed to going out to work and looking after her own home.

'After I have done that I don't seem to have much energy left over for other things. Perhaps all one can do is to be friendly and helpful. The New Testament says we have got different gifts. There is teaching and preaching and leadership, but there are also the gifts of helping and showing mercy and giving. Then there is the ministry of prayer and the ministry of financial support, which a single woman can certainly do because she hasn't got dependents.

'Sometimes I feel very negative about it, but that's when I'm thinking selfishly or when I am getting panic-stricken about being fifty and feeling that I've done nothing in life. Then I come back to the fact that all that really matters is that our names are written in heaven. But we are actually responsible for what we are doing in life, and I do feel terribly useless. I believe it's part of the discipline that God has given me this particular job to do. I would rather be doing what I would regard as more holy and more directly helpful to people, but I believe that God has put me where I am, and I have to keep telling myself that.'

I reminded Rosemary that when we had talked before she had said that she didn't feel valued in the church because she was a woman and a single woman. She said she thought it was right that the emphasis should be on the importance of the Christian home and the importance of bringing up children, because this is an area that is under threat at the moment. 'But,' she went on, 'there is a danger of overlooking the fact that unmarried women in our society need help to see their role and their value, because otherwise they will go the way of the feminists, and get thoroughly irate.'

I asked her what she perceived her own role to be, and she told me, 'I am truly perplexed about the whole thing. I wonder why I am not doing more useful things.' So then I asked her what could be done, or what could she do, for single Christian women in the church who feel that secular and Christian society sees the best as being married and bringing up children? What is our value in the sight of God?

'I think we have to emphasise the value of the Christian family today because this is under attack. So I would put that first because I know many Christian families who are greatly troubled, and have problems with temptations in their own relations with each other. It is shouted at us from every newspaper that if a woman hasn't a job she isn't doing what she should be doing and if she's at home looking after the kids then she is only half-fulfilled. I think this has to be strongly resisted.'

At this point I said, 'But this book isn't about married women!'

'No,' Rosemary agreed. 'But it is interesting so far as single women are concerned that one of the teaching staff came up to me just last week and said, "I expect that as a woman you feel undervalued at work." I said, "No, I don't, because I have a respect for my colleagues and the work they do; and whether they are men or women is irrelevant. I don't feel at all that they undervalue me because I am a woman."

'There is no problem at all at work. There never has been. It's in the church—where I think it is Satan getting at me and my own selfishness. I don't think that women are to take positions of authority in the church. So they have to wait to see what God wants them to do. And being women is the great thing.'

So I asked Rosemary, 'Why haven't you got any value? You say it's the work of Satan. What is it that would give you value?' She was doubtful about the question.

'Isn't it selfish for me to think in terms of value?' I totally disagreed with her, and said so (and just as she values her conversations with friends so do I—and I especially value the conversations that Rosemary and I have together, in which we can disagree with each other, but in great courtesy and respect).

'No!' I said. 'I think that's utterly wrong. We all enormously need a sense of our own value. What about that lovely prayer "The Lord bless you and keep you: the Lord make his face to shine upon you, and be gracious to you: the Lord lift up his countenance upon you, and give you peace" (Num 6:24–26). That's about looking into the face of God and knowing that we are precious. It's the transforming face of God that changes a person. Bishop John Robinson said that to look at Jesus was to see the human face of God—and people knew that Jesus valued them.'

'But that's something internal,' argued Rosemary. 'It's nothing to do with the value that other people give to us. It is one's own relationship with God that is the all-important thing, and that is where the sense of real value would come from.'

'But supposing,' I asked, 'that some single women came to you and said, "We really feel second class citizens in the church." How would you help them not to feel that? What could you do to ease their pain? Because I don't believe they are meant to have that pain, and a lot of them have got it. So what could you do?'

Rosemary looked profoundly thoughtful. 'I think we just have to battle it out for ourselves. We all have to say to ourselves "I know that I am valuable to God, because I am his child—and he must so enrich me in my relationship with him, and so help me to seek him, that I shall know the inner satisfaction I need." I don't think it's about putting things on the outside and decorating the outside with activities. That may pander to one's own self esteem, but I don't think it has anything to do with spiritual things—which is what you are talking about.'

I agreed with her about that. 'Yes, it's not doing—it's being.'

'The minister has been preaching on Malachi recently,' Rosemary told me. "They shall be mine," says the Lord, "in the day that I make up my jewels . . ." (Mal 3:17 AV), and that is about our value. If we only had a real sense of how great the privilege is of being a child of God—and such we are—then the outward would become better. It would become serener and brighter and more valuable!'

I asked Rosemary my final question. 'Do you think that married people are going to be brighter jewels in the crown?' She gave me a very passionate answer. 'Not at all! Because I think 1 Corinthians 7 teaches very clearly that the single life has a particular and peculiar value and that it is certainly not to be regarded as inferior to the married life.'

Dr Helen King

Helen King is a lecturer in history at St Katharine's College, Liverpool. She is also a member of various boards and bodies: the General Synod of the Church of England; the British Council of Churches Assembly; the Board of Division of Community Affairs of BCC; and the Ecumenical Forum of European Christian Women. She has written numerous articles on Ancient Greek medicine and mythology, and she likes the theatre, science fiction, and gardening.

Helen happens to be exceptionally clever, a fact which one member of her family saw as a distinct disadvantage. 'When I went to Newnham as a Research Fellow my granny said, "Bang go your marriage prospects,"'! But there was a theological college just opposite which was almost entirely male and that made her feel a lot better.'

When Helen was at school she didn't want to go to university. 'I didn't want the competition,' she admitted, 'endlessly trying to be top. I was quite good at being top, but once you are top there's only one direction you can go. Down! So that puts you under a lot of personal strain. And there's a general feeling around that it's not the thing to be a clever girl.

'My first year at university was fun, because no one knew how good I was. But then I did horribly well in the history exam and people were a bit shocked, because I don't think anyone had ever managed to get a first in their first year exams and I did. But I felt, "Here I go again. I've got to struggle to live up to people's expectations and keep being top." I got a first in my finals, and I'm the only person who ever did on that particular course, because it's an absolute killer.

'After I got my degree I did my PhD in London on the ancient Greek concept of time. Everyone thought it meant clocks and calendars, but it didn't—although I wasn't very sure what it did mean. I was interested in the whole idea of time and questions like "What do words about time tell you?" But I gradually got down to looking at time in the life-cycle and how different stages in one's life are represented. It meant looking at how the Greeks saw themselves in relation to the gods and to the beasts, and how they defined themselves. I was curious to know what it meant to be a woman in that society, because when they talked about the relationship between god, man and beast they really did mean man. Not men and women. Males. Women were in a different category, somewhere down with the beasts.'

I wondered if Helen liked being a woman, and she said, 'Yes, I never wanted to be a man. It's much easier to be in the underclass, and I think we are.'

'Do you think we are second class citizens?' I asked.

'Definitely. Look at Oxford and Cambridge. The colleges which have gone mixed that were originally all male have got women undergraduates now. But most lecturers are still male. If you look at most women's *curriculum vitae* they have odd gaps where they have had children or because their husband moved. If their husband gets a job in the university they might only be able to do just a little teaching, and since they can't get a proper academic job in the new place they do part time work or get paid by the hour. So their CV's don't look so good.

'A lot of my married friends have that problem. One of the things I like about being single is the freedom it gives me, and I don't have to go through the anguish I see them going through with their job and their children. When I do academic research I am on a short contract of up to three years. But I can just take off and go wherever it is, and I have my firm family base to come back to.

'Another thing about being single is that I like being on my own. I wouldn't like having someone around all the time. I like to collapse at the end of a hard day and let the thoughts of what I have been researching go round in my mind—without having to think all the time about a husband who has had a hard day's work and wants to talk to me! I like the freedom to think about who I am, without having to support someone else who doesn't know who he is!'

So I asked Helen if she had discovered who she was. 'I'm getting close. I relate to the Prince of Wales in his attempt to discover who he is. I'm quite strong. I'm quite keen on being up front. I like to display myself publicly. That sounds awful, doesn't it, I ought to blush. I like to have a role which gives me quite a lot of public exposure and a lot of contact with people. That sounds dire, but I like to be at the centre of things.

'Somebody sent me along once to a child psychologist and he said, "You're tall, aren't you? How do you feel about that?" I said, "It's nice. When I'm in a crowd I can see over other people's heads," and he said, "Ah, you like being on top of people! You like being above them!" But I said, "No! I just like seeing over their heads in crowds!" It's tricky, but I don't think I'm a secret dictator.'

I said to Helen that I had heard someone say that the moment we stop wanting to display ourselves and show off we're finished, and we're fooling ourselves if we say that we don't want to. She agreed. 'Yes, maybe we can be honest about the fact that we like it.' So then I asked her what it is that she wants them to see about her. She told me, 'I want them to see that I'm single and that I'm chaste. I think that's something very positive, and in this society to be single and chaste is supposed to be fairly rare. I'm a virgin, and I haven't been brought up to be ashamed of that fact. Once people know me well enough for me to say 'That's how I live' they really seem to approve of it and they say that's how they think it ought to be.

'But a lot of them assume that I won't be single for very much longer. People say, "It's all very well talking about chastity on the Synod, Helen: Mr Right will come along, and then you won't be able to talk about it." At the Synod recently someone mentioned the statistic which says there will soon be a surplus of males in the twenty-one to thirty-five age group. So people said, "There you are! He'll be coming along soon!". I despair, and I have an awful vision of a fairy tale scenario in which Mr Right gallops along on his white charger. But I don't think that the person I'm looking for is ever going to turn up!'

I felt just the same as Helen, and told her that I am looking for a theologian who is fantastic at sex and thinks I'm marvellous.

'But think of having to discuss theology at dinner every night!'

'I could discuss theology in bed!' I told her.

She grinned. 'That's obviously why you want that combination!'

Then I asked Helen to tell me what she felt about being a woman in the church, and she said 'I'm one of those women in the church who have said "Why can't women be sidesmen?" I have been given the answer "But that's silly, we've got enough men. Why do we need women sidesmen?" Followed by, "If you want to help, you can make the coffee." That was seven years ago (and you should just try to drink my coffee!). Being a sidesman was a male role. It took me years before I realised that women could be, and then I turned up at the elections armed with a copy of the church representation rules with the right bit underlined in case anyone tried to query it.

'Another woman became a sidesman at the same meeting, once she had realised there was nothing to stop her. But then they said, "The books are so heavy. You won't be able to carry them round the church." And I said, "Come on! I worked in a library on Saturday for years, and I've carried armfuls of heavy books"! It's an interesting role being a sidesman, because it's got the feminine qualities of welcoming and greeting.'

'What would you like to see changed in our society?' I asked. 'Our attitude to sex,' said Helen. 'The view that sex is something recreational. Everybody does it—and if you don't that's the end of you. That was the attitude of the ancient Greeks: if you don't do it you are liable to fall down dead or be dreadfully ill. You will be totally unhappy and unfulfilled. I think this whole attitude is utterly appalling, and I think we have got to hit back and fight it.'

I wondered what she thought wholeness would be for us. 'Wholeness would be the acceptance of women as women. Not trying to make us into men. I feel convinced that there should be a definition of the feminine which isn't also a negative definition. Because as soon as you define something as masculine then the opposite becomes feminine, and the goody ones all end up on the male side and the baddy ones all end up on the female side. It's the whole classification of opposites, and one sex ends up with all the negative bits.'

'But what if you take things like gentleness and caring?' I queried. 'Are they female? Or are they female because they just happen, and aggression and force and violence are appropriate to the male?

'But then,' I argued, 'you could say that strength and initiative were also feminine qualities. I think we have got ourselves into a difficulty and got confused with roles.'

Helen continued with this line of thought. 'There is also the point that if you say certain qualities are feminine you've got a problem, because some individuals won't display those qualities as much as other individuals. So you run the risk of saying that certain people are not OK because they're not feminine.'

I said that I believe God has made us male and female in the image of God. He didn't make us hermaphrodites. I like what Jung says, that a man needs to get in touch with the feminine in his nature (the *anima*) and a woman needs to come to terms with the masculine within her. If we don't learn to use our inner drive it will control us, but once we are in touch with it we can use it like a car engine. I know that when I got in touch with my own inner aggression I became far more creative. Now I use the aggression within me to drive with (rather than it driving me) and I think I have become more of a woman in the process.

Helen agreed. 'Yes, and I think it is significant that when you asked me who I was the first thing I said was, "I'm strong". That is important, because it isn't something that you want to admit at an early stage of your life. To be strong is bad. It's masculine. But even once you know that's how you are it doesn't mean you are permanently strong. You are perfectly capable of bursting into tears and breaking down and screaming. But perhaps it is because you are able to do that that you might have got somewhere near wholeness.'

Dr Ruth Fowke

Dr Ruth Fowke is a consultant psychiatrist. She has written several popular and very helpful books, *Coping with Crises*, *Growing through Crises* and *Beginning Pastoral Counselling*, and she has contributed chapters to *We believe in Healing* and *Keeping a Spiritual Journal*. She likes to see new places and have new experiences (but 'in moderation!') and her great interest is her own garden and also other people's gardens.

I wasn't able to see much of her garden, because when I went to interview her it was dark. But she had put the light on outside her front door to welcome me, and there was light shining out of the windows as I walked up the path. She opened the door as soon as I rang, and settled me down in a large, comfortable chair in her large, comfortable sitting room. We started off by getting to know each other a bit, and then started the interview.

I asked Ruth if she liked being single, and she said, 'Yes, some of the time I do, particularly when I have been dealing with some marital problem—or when I want to go off and do my own thing, like suddenly taking a holiday. I can phone up a friend just at a whim and off we go. If you are married you can't do that.

'There are other times, though, when I feel a sense of aloneness and I am very aware of being alone. But I am not sure that marriage is the answer to that, and it isn't only marriage which would fulfill that need. A wide circle of friends could fulfill it.

'After those recent gales we had I was very heartened when one friend came round to ask, "Did anything happen to you? Are you all right?" And someone else phoned up to tell me not to try and go out because she had just

42

heard that the road was blocked at both ends. I don't think I would have known how to cope with the emergency—it was too much to cope with on my own. But that could just as well be true of a couple if they are not handy or practical!'

I wondered what Ruth most liked about being single, and she was very clear about her answer. 'Freedom! Freedom! Freedom! And quietness! Being uninterrupted. I really like not having to think of anyone else in the morning, although I know couples could come to that arrangement, and some do. First thing in the morning they never exchange a word. I depends whether you marry like or contra, doesn't it?

'I suppose the word "freedom" sums it up. There are just so many things I can do. I can *not* make up my mind, and I can change it as often as I like.'

From our conversation before starting the interview I realised that Ruth had a wide circle of friends, so I asked her how she entertained them. She said she doesn't like crowds. She experimented once with another single friend and they had invited round a crowd of about fifteen to twenty, but she hadn't enjoyed it. She preferred to have two people at a time, or at the most three. She had also experimented with inviting two couples, but still preferred to have people a few at a time, because it suited her personally.

'It isn't necessarily the done thing,' she said, 'but it's what I like. I get on with people, and the fewer the better. If there are a lot I find myself distracted. There is a bit going on here and a bit going on somewhere else— even at the meal table.'

I wanted to ask Ruth a very important question, because I felt that in her professional capacity as a consultant psychiatrist she could give a really satisfactory answer. I wanted to know whether she thought it was possible for a single person to be a whole person.

'Yes, I do,' she said, 'and I think sometimes more

whole. But then perhaps I am prejudiced because of the number of un-whole people I see. Married or single people, who can't make up their own minds and who are always living in the shadow of someone else, whether it's husband or children or parents, even if they're aged fifty or sixty. They have never really become their own person.

'We shouldn't live in anybody's shadow. What I mean by that is always doing what someone else wants or expects. It is perpetuating what happens in childhood. In pre-school years children are expected to do what mummy wants. A wise mother lets them develop their own inclinations, but not all parents do that and they squash out the child who is temperamentally different from the parent.

'I used to be discouraged from daydreaming. "Come along! Hurry up!" is what I remember from my childhood, because by nature I suppose I am more dreamy and less practical. I certainly remember that refrain, "Stop daydreaming!" There is a time and a place to be told that—but it is destructive to have it drummed into you all the time.

'It also depends on what school you go to whether you can become your own person, and how successful your teenage rebellion is and whether it goes through to a reasonable conclusion.

'Then some people go into authoritarian jobs where they are always pleasing the boss or keeping the rules. Or it doesn't have to be a person that they are subservient to. It can be the job itself—hence some of the problem when people lose their jobs: "Who am I? Who do I belong to?"

'Some people's whole identity is in their children, and sometimes we see the perpetuation of a very matriarchal family. The mother has difficulty in letting the children go. Life can revolve around things like "Who's coming for Christmas?", or even the family business, or helping one another out. And that is fine and healthy to some extent, but when does it go over to being unhealthy? It's not a question of black and white. It's infinite shades of grey.

'Then you get the mother who falls apart when the last child leaves. Or the children who can't cope with mum except by no longer keeping in contact. These are the sorts of people that I come in contact with and they are very sad. They get into all sorts of problems because they are trying to let the children go and emotionally they can't—so the children keep mother at arm's length and ensure less and less contact.'

I was very aware that many single women were caught up in the sort of situations that Ruth was describing: the single woman who had never managed to break free emotionally, or the single woman who had ended up looking after her old mother or old father. The other children in the family were happily married (or even miserably married: that wasn't the point). But because they were married they were not prepared to help, and they simply assumed that because the single woman was on her own it was her job to look after the aged parent. I asked Ruth what she would say to someone in that situation, and whether she thought that sort of self-sacrifice was as it was meant to be.

'No,' she said, 'I don't at all. But I think the roots of it are so much earlier. If people make a break, so that they become their own person, then whether or not they actually live together with a parent doesn't matter. Because they can be just as tied if they are at the other end of the country. They are always phoning up. They are very neurotic because they are not doing what mother wants—even though they may be married and physically separated.

'It is not to do with being single or married. It is to do with their own development. I think the saddest people are those who at mid-life, or even later, are still looking after old people *if the relationship isn't right*.

'What matters is the quality of the relationship and the maturity of the relationship. It doesn't have to be parents. It can be unmarried siblings living together. Brothers and sisters, or two sisters—and one dominates the other. Or maybe neither of them can actually do what is right for them, because they don't want to displease or upset the other. I haven't come across too many of those, but I do know a few. I am not saying that none of these people should live together. But it's like steering a boat through the rapids—and the boat can be steered.'

I imagined that Ruth occasionally felt lonely, like the rest of us, so I asked her how she coped when she did. She said: 'The first thing is to recognise that I am lonely. It can take many forms. I may not immediately know it's loneliness. So I have to identify it and then do something about it. There are various clues. Perhaps I am ill at ease, or getting irritable over silly things. Or I keep eating. I can be doing those things because I am hurting about something else, but it can often be loneliness.

'Perhaps I have taken some time off to be alone and write. I like a lot of aloneness, but I don't want too much, and I can find myself munching away at chocolate bars when I am either stuck at my writing or lacking in company. Or it may be both those things have happened together.

'Once I have identified my condition as loneliness I would probably use the phone a lot. Either I would have a conversation with a friend or I might arrange to go out and do something, though not necessarily on that day. Sometimes I might just phone up and say "Hey, can I come round?", or "Would you like lunch today?", or tomorrow, or whenever.

'I remember that one August I phoned about six people and there was nobody in. (Which is not unusual, because August is a very empty month, with a lot of people away.) That sort of thing is not just my experience, I hear it from other people. So I think the only answer is to have a diverse and wide range of contacts and to be prepared for people to say "No"—and not to be put off after the first one.'

I wondered what Ruth did with all this in her relationship with God, so I asked her how she prayed both in her loneliness and her singleness. She told me: 'I can't do other than take it to the Lord and say "This is me," a bit like *Mr God, this is Anna*.[5] Sometimes I say, "This is me and this is where I am. . . ." And I just take it from there. I can't do otherwise.

'I might have an argument with God. I might say, "Is this all you've got for me?" But usually I think it's a spur for me to be seeking greater intimacy with him. Again, having identified what's wrong, I would just say to the Lord, "I am needing company, or friendship, or fellowship." I would somehow explore it with him, and then ask him to fill that vacuum. I would say, "I am a social creature, and you chose to make me like this. Come on! What are you going to do about it? What are *you* going to do about it and what do you want *me* to do about it?" I don't think I can separate those things.'

When I am feeling angry about my situation I thump things and say to God "I'm fed up!" ' So I asked Ruth if she ever got angry and did things like that. She said she did. 'Right! Thump a cushion! It's better than a hard chair. Oh yes, I do get angry. Mostly when I am like that I do it when I'm walking. I will walk furiously over the hills—mainly when I am on a retreat and various things have come out.

'My big temptation is to lose myself in other activities, or just watch television. "I need some relaxation," I'll say to myself, and three hours later I am still watching some drivel. Or else I go to the other extreme and I'm busy. I've got a house and a garden and there are always a thousand things that I can be doing.'

Ruth had told me that she goes on retreat, and since for some of us this is a new and an unexplored area of spirituality I asked her to say something about it.

'I actually have a Roman Catholic spiritual director,' Ruth told me. 'I go to the Cenacle Retreat House at Hindhead. I think the point of a retreat is to enter into a relationship with God without any distraction. I was terrified to begin with, so I did a very slow, dipping my toe in thing to start with.

'I went for a short weekend, and then a longer weekend, and then six days and then eight. But I was terrified. Because I always surround myself with books and things. And then to be alone with nothing but the Bible! I cheated—I took a radio and a Reader's Digest. But I think the instructions were not to take anything.

'The first time I was there I just assumed that one shouldn't go out of the grounds, but I was wrong. After that I had great fun walking. When I had exhausted the local common I really felt daring, going off as far as Frensham Ponds, which is my favourite place. It's quite beautiful and there is the space to stride out.

'The benefit of a retreat is first of all to be without distractions, and secondly to be able to talk with somebody who actually understands. I hadn't come across that before, and I think it is a sad lack in the Evangelical wing of the Church.'

I was interested to know what sort of prayer Ruth found helpful, and whether she used silence at all. She said she did: 'A lot of silence. At times the majority of my prayer is silence. It is very much less intercession. I find myself a bit guilty when the prayer lists come from the various societies, because most of them just go in the wastepaper-basket. If a person comes into my mind then obviously I will go along with that and pray for them, and if I am interceding it can often be in the car. I have often thought I should organise my car journeys and have my little prayer lists there. But I am not an organised person, so that would be doing violence to me.

'Sometimes I pray in tongues. Very little. I'm not disciplined about it. Do you know the advice to Jackie

Pullinger? She was advised to pray for ten minutes every day in tongues, and it wasn't until she began that discipline that her work took off. I have sometimes thought about that. I will turn to tongues if I am feeling really stuck or if it comes naturally. Those are the only times. But it doesn't form a normal part of my praying.'

I asked Ruth if there was anything she wanted to say that I hadn't already asked her, and she said 'Yes. When you wrote to me you said that one of the things this book was going to be about was how to be a successful single woman, and that sounded to me like a career book. So I wondered if you would consider altering it, because I thought "Oh dear, what about those who *aren't* successful?" I think what you are really wanting to talk about is being successful at being a single woman. And that is about being comfortable with being single.

'The question we really have to ask is "How can I be a success as a woman—whether I am married or single?" It's like Jeremiah's potter, isn't it? We don't choose the type of clay. "Cannot the potter do with me as he chooses?" And if he happens to have chosen me to be a woman rather than a man then it means he wants me to be a success as a *woman*.'

Joyce Blackwell

When I finally knocked at Joyce Blackwell's front door (over an hour late because I had got lost earlier in the evening) she welcomed me inside and made me feel at home and at ease. She lives in a pretty, modern house in Godalming, and is the Head Teacher of Bramley Church of England First School. For ten years she was the editor of an annual directory of an engineering trade association, and when her children were in Primary School she trained as a mature student at Gipsy Hill College of Education. She likes singing, walking, playing badminton, doing needlework, travelling (she leads Highway Holiday Houseparties on the continent) and playing scrabble.

Joyce and her husband Len had two sons, but some years ago Len died, so she is a widow. I asked her to tell me about her widowhood—a very common form of being 'a single woman'—and how she has coped with her sadness and bereavement.

'One of the things I had to learn was the healing power of tears. I had to accept that tears had a healing property that the Lord gives, and that anger has too. But I didn't discover that I was angry until five years after my husband died.

'Five of us had gone to a creativity weekend at the Dodnor Sailing Centre on the Isle of Wight. We were all women. Two of us were widows, and the other three had left their husbands behind at home.

'At the weekend there were various groups you could join: writing and craft, and drama and music, and I was in those two. In the drama we were given the question "What did Jesus do on Easter Sunday?", and you can imagine the theological things that came out of that.

'We eventually formed into different groups to act out different attitudes: a "poor me" group, a group that ridiculed Jesus, and an "anger" group, which I was in. I don't know how I got in it but I did, and I think that it was in acting it out that I got in touch with feelings I had hadn't realised were there. I had simply never been aware that I was angry, although this was five years after Len died.

'There is one thing about bereavement which no one ever told me, and I don't think I have ever seen it written. People think "Oh, in a year or two she'll be over it." But that isn't true. It takes a long, long time, much longer than people imagine. In some ways the gap is always there—it's like a scar. It improves, but you are always left with it. I think this is something that very few people realise, unless they have experienced it them-selves.

'I know that for the first six months I walked around as though I was only half of me. The other half was lost. Although many of the people within the fellowship of St John's, Woking, surrounded us with their love, prayers and practical help, it was very difficult for my children, and I still wonder how much it has damaged them. I can't do anything about it, and all I can do is to trust that the Lord will heal the places that need to be healed, and somehow make up the things that they have obviously missed out on.

'There's another thing too that people never seem to talk about, which is that you have a good sexual relation-ship and then it's suddenly cut off—and that's the end of it. Nobody ever talks about that. And at the same time you lose the person who has been interested in all the little details of your life.

'That's why I so value a friend of mine called Mar-garet, a teacher who lives in Lancashire. She had suf-fered a broken romance during a period she was about to have a heart operation. At the very time she needed someone he just threw her over. However, we see our meeting and subsequent friendship as God's compensation. We have travelled extensively, and even fulfilled her lifelong ambition to fly through the Grand Canyon: with Margaret's heart condition an almost impossible dream. We have been very good for each other, and the Lord has given us tremendous conversations. As our relationship grows our spiritual life deepens too, and God has been able to use us both in his service in a different way.

'I wondered whether I would meet anyone to re-marry. Several people have said to me, "I can't understand why you haven't married again," and I have said, "Well, the Lord hasn't sent me anyone whom I have felt is right." And I am sure one would feel it was right. But I'm not sure now whether I would re-marry. Sometimes I think that perhaps it would be nice, or sometimes I think I don't want to bother again. But the possibility is always there if that's what the Lord wants.

'Len had only been a Christian for eight years before he died, and in those years he grew at a most tremendous pace. He went up to Wembley and was a counsellor with the Billy Graham Campaign, and it was wonderful to see him grow. He could see the power of prayer much clearer than many Christians do, because I don't think that a lot of them really do see it.

'He had a book called *A Kind of Praying*, which he hadn't had very long, and after he died I used it. Then Tony Waite, the Vicar, gave me a *Daily Light* and Oswald Chambers' *My Utmost for His Highest*. Often in one of those books there was just a pinpoint there to let me know that the Lord was absolutely holding me up.

'We also had a weekly prayer meeting at the church, and that was another place where I learned the power of tears. It was incredible. I used to pray a prayer, and then another person used to pray a prayer, and then for the rest of the time I just sat there with tears streaming down my face. It was really odd. Prayers about anything at all just seemed to trigger it off. And I thought, "Well, the Lord obviously realises I find it difficult to cry—and this is one place where I must feel safe enough to be able to."

'I am an optimistic person on the whole, but I do get down just occasionally. I can remember it happening in the year which would have been our twenty-fifth wedding anniversary. My eldest son went off and got himself an apprenticeship in Coventry when he was eighteen, and I didn't hear from him for three weeks. It was just like another bereavement all over again, and I really went downhill for a whole month. It was a bad time. But it is wonderful how the Lord lifts you out of it.

'Something you realise as your children grow up is that you have to make a life of your own. In my view that's very important. You can't live your children's lives—they are independent people. You may be hurt because they don't realise how you feel. My two sons are beginning to realise now, because they are getting older, but at the time they don't know when they are trampling all over your feelings. They are in and out of the house, and it's like a hotel—and you are like a chauffeur. This happens in ordinary families as well, but I think that as a widow or a single parent family you are a little more vulnerable. Because you haven't got anybody to say it to you can't say: "Oh, isn't it awful! Kids!" So you just have to take it. When I think now of the number of times I've trundled up to Nottingham! Twenty-six journeys I made, up and down, bringing all my son's stuff backwards and forwards. There's no one else to do it so you have to.

'My eldest son's got a flat now in London, and the other day he said to me "Oh, it's such hard work—when you're out at work all day and then you've got to come home and start painting." And I said, "Yes dear, I do know! I did that—and the garden and the family. I went out to work as well!" And it's beginning to dawn, now he is actually running his own home—he's suddenly realising what it's like!

'But they don't realise it at the time, and you have simply got to be prepared to be hurt. I kept reminding myself I had brought them up to be independent, especially when the younger one went off to the States at eighteen for his higher education. Quite honestly I don't know how non-Christians manage. I am sure it was my trust in God that saw me through all that. When Len died, God's guiding into an unsought for teaching career eight years before made sense. It was like seeing the pieces of a jigsaw fit together, and over and above all my sadness, I was left with a sense of awe.

'But I think you have got to step out in faith and trust the Lord. That's what I did when I moved. I thought "I'm working now at Bramley. I'm going to be there till I retire, and I'm not getting any younger." And although it was a reasonable drive I had to come through Guildford every day. I felt I should push the door with a view to moving. Quite a saga, but as always God's timing is perfect, and I know I am in the right house, in the right place, and within the right church fellowship for the present.'

Doreen Ayling

Doreen Ayling is a widow with two adult daughters, her husband having died six years ago after they had been married for twenty-five years. As a mature student she trained to be a teacher and taught for thirteen years in Hampshire. Before that she had worked for many years as a private secretary, and in 1984 she came to Durham to act as Ruth Etchells' personal assistant. She likes music, the theatre, and the countryside.

I began our interview by saying to her, 'Apart from the bereavement, and the awful feeling of loss, did it feel strange to be on your own?' 'Yes,' she said. 'Very strange. It is difficult to describe what it was like to be on my own after being married for nearly twenty-five years.

'As marriages go ours was extremely happy. I don't mean that we never had any arguments, but we were very happily married for ninety-nine per cent of the time. And when you have that kind of relationship your roots grow together. So it was as if part of me was wrenched away. When you divide plants the roots of the two halves are all tangled up, and in the same way, in marriage, your lives have grown together. So when you lose a partner whom you have loved deeply then your own roots are torn—and they bleed.

'I think there were several reasons why I was able to cope. I was very fortunate in my family. I have two daughters who are grown up, and they are a source of great joy. When my husband died they were sitting their finals at university, but they were tremendously supportive and they still are. The young man who was to become my son-in-law, and was then my daughter's boyfriend, was equally supportive. So I was extremely fortunate in my family.

'Another thing was that we had been very much part of the parish church. My husband was church warden when he died, and the family of the church were incredibly marvellous to me. They were enormously loving and warm, and I can't tell you how much it meant or how much they did for me. They weren't only supportive at the time of his death. They went on being so, and they still are.

'So I was extraordinarily fortunate, and I know I wouldn't have coped nearly so well if it hadn't been for those two wonderful things. I am lucky, too, in that I do have a deep faith.'

I said to Doreen that some widows feel they move into a sort of no-man's land and that the whole of their social life changes. I wondered if she had experienced that. She said that to start with she hadn't: 'At the time of my husband's death people were careful to include me in everything, and I was just wrapped around, so I wasn't conscious of any lack at all then. But more recently, when I moved to Durham, that changed. Very few people knew me, and I found it subtly different.

'I suppose in some ways a widow is like a divorcee. She is invited into the large groups but not asked to dinner parties. I think it's partly that they don't quite know what to do with an odd woman. People are wonderfully kind and friendly, but there is that slight barrier.

'When I am entertaining I have married couples as well as single people. I try to keep the numbers reasonably balanced and I usually invite another single woman to balance the group. I have a mixture of married people and single people, and it works quite well.'

I wondered if Doreen had experienced any practical difficulties in being on her own and she said that she had, but that she was adjusting. 'My husband and I used to work very much as a team. I did certain things for him some of the time and he did certain things for me. I looked after domestic things rather more than the young people do now, and he looked after the car—the tax and that kind of thing. Then suddenly I had to learn to do all the things for myself or else pay for help. I found that a bit of a nuisance but it wasn't a great problem. When my husband died my whole circumstances changed. Until that time we had been a family of four all living together. The girls were at home in the vacation. But just as he died they set out into the world. So I suddenly changed from being a family of four into just being me.

'I found it a bit difficult to sort things out for myself. I tried to be really independent and self-supporting and not to call on too many friends. And financially it was very hard but it's not as bad now as it was at the beginning.

'I have been very fortunate. When my husband died I was teaching, and I carried on teaching for two years. Then this completely new job as Ruth Etchells' secretary came along quite unexpectedly, and opened up a whole new career and way of life.

'I went back to being a secretary, and this opportunity of working for Ruth Etchells was heaven sent. That's the only way I can describe it. God just gave me this right out of the blue, and I have been so fortunate and so blessed in my job. It has been a tremendous privilege to work not only for Ruth Etchells but also for St John's College. So I have really had very little to grumble about. I have been very, very lucky.'

I wondered whether Doreen ever got depressed, and how she prayed if she really felt desolate. 'Occasionally I get depressed,' she admitted. 'Everyone does. But I think the hardest thing to bear about depression is the fact that really one has no right to be depressed. But obviously one gets that way and then the only thing to do is to put it before the Lord. There is help there. And one comes out of it.

'One of the most uplifting and comforting people to read—and I read her over and over again—is Mother Julian. I didn't discover her until after my husband died. One of my daughters had been at university in Norwich, and we went back there for her on a sentimental journey, and she took me to the little chapel of Mother Julian. It was there that I picked up her writings and I find them an enormous comfort. I love all that she has written, but there are two passages in particular that are very special:

We Shall Not Be Overcome

Though we are in such pain, trouble and distress, that it seems to us that we are unable to think of anything except how we are and what we feel, yet as soon as we may, we are to pass lightly over it, and count it as nothing. And why? Because God wills that we should understand that if we know him and love him and reverently fear him, we shall have rest and be at peace. And we shall rejoice in all that he does.

I understood truly that our soul may never find rest in things below, but when it looks through all created things to find its self, it must never remain gazing on its self, but feast on the sight of God its maker who lives within.

He did not say, 'You shall not be tempest-tossed, you shall not be work-weary, you shall not be discomforted.' But he said, 'You shall not be overcome.' God wants us to heed these words so that we shall always be strong in trust, both in sorrow and in joy.

The Strength of Humility

He says, 'Do not blame yourself too much, thinking that your trouble and distress is all your fault. For it is not my will that you should be unduly sad and despondent.'

Our enemy tries to depress us by false fears which he proposes. His intention is to make us so weary and dejected, that we let the blessed sight of our everlasting friend slip from our minds.

It is a beautiful humility—brought about by the grace and mercy of the Holy Spirit—when a sinful soul willingly and gladly accepts the chastisement our Lord himself would give us. It will seem light and easy, if only we will accept contentedly what he calls upon us to bear.[6]

Mother Frances Dominica

Frances Dominica is the Superior of the All Saints Community and the founder of Helen House, in Oxford—the first hospice in the world for children. It grew out of the special friendship that Frances Dominica and the community had with a little girl called Helen, who was gravely ill and helpless after a brain tumour, and with her family. The community decided to extend that friendship to other gravely ill children and their families.

When I first interviewed Frances Dominica in Helen House, four years ago and on the subject of dying, there were several small interruptions, as a child happily insisted on coming into the room where we sat to say hello to Mother Frances. Outside in the garden a dog explored the lawn and the flower borders.

This time there were no interruptions, but still the same feeling of happiness and being at home in a safe and loving place. This interview is actually one which Frances Dominica has given me for one of the Bible Reading Fellowship's books. But it is so relevant to the Christian single woman that I am also including it here. It is in a slightly different form from the other interviews.

Chastity and the love of God

Chastity is for all Christians. Far from being a denial of our humanity it is an affirmation of our truest selves. It is strong, pure, honest and single-minded.

Chastity requires an integrity which does not use the other person for our own gain or gratification but respects the other's dignity and freedom as a child of God. It is sensitive to the other person's greatest good.

Chastity is an acknowledgement of the unique relationship of love we have with God. The word is sometimes confused with celibacy. For a monk or a nun celibacy is implicit in the vow of chastity, and means we choose not to marry.

There are two separate things: chastity, to which all Christians are called, and celibacy, to which some are called, including those who take Religious Vows.

To choose the celibate way is not to deny the goodness or the beauty of marriage or the potential for growth and holiness in marriage, but it is to recognise that God calls some people to remain unmarried in order to be free for the purposes he ordains. It doesn't mean that if you are married you cannot be free for God's purposes, but just that there are different callings. The first meaning of the word 'chaste' in the Shorter Oxford Dictionary is 'Pure from unlawful, sexual intercourse, continent.' Chaste love has got to be built on a relationship of love with God, otherwise it has no sure or solid foundation. Even in a very close bond of marriage, the two individuals involved each have to have space for their own unique relationship with God. They cannot become totally one person, however close their relationship is.

It has often been said that there is a space in each one of us which is God-shaped, and only God can fill it. No one can be totally possessed by another. There is a part which is for God alone.

I believe that chaste loving in a marriage or in any other relationship springs from the recognition of this truth. Chaste love recognises the other person as a child of God first and foremost, before claiming anything from the beloved.

The relationship should be trusting enough to enable growth in the two people, never a possessive, suffocating thing. It should bring about a freedom to grow in holiness as God guides and enables.

Often when you talk about chastity people say, 'Oh,

chastity means no sex.' But that is not what Christian chastity means, either within or outside marriage. Our sexuality is an integral part of each one of us and has its expression to a greater or lesser degree in all our relationships. It is one of God's loveliest gifts to us. But as with all things of infinite beauty that are given to us, we can so easily spoil, abuse and destroy. The deepest love is chaste because it is concerned for the greatest good of the other, even if that means costly self-discipline and the courage to deny ourselves immediate pleasure or gratification.

As we become more chaste so we become more beautiful, more lovable and more ready to love unconditionally, because we begin to resemble the God in whose image and likeness we are made.

The Reverend Patsy Kettle

Patsy Kettle is the curate of Wonersh Parish Church. Her family now consists of one husband, two step-daughters, four step-grandchildren, one sister, two nephews, one niece and one dog. She was a primary school teacher for five years, and then spent twenty years in parish ministry as a parish worker. She likes gardening and birdwatching, and does calligraphy. She writes for Scripture Union's *Alive to God* Notes, and has written *What? Me a Housegroup Leader?* and *Staying Sane Under Stress*.

When I finally arrived to interview her, forty-five minutes late, Patsy was standing outside her house looking for me. It was a winter evening, and I had got dismally lost in the wilds of Surrey (which I have always thought is the worst signposted county in England!), with the cars behind pushing so close, and the headlights of the cars in front battering my windscreen so fiercely, that there was no way to check such signposts as there were. One of the practical disadvantages of being a single person is that you usually have to find the way to places on your own, without a map reader!

I was feeling hassled and rather sorry for myself—but Patsy somehow put things right fairly fast. *Staying Sane Under Stress* had obviously been written from her heart and wasn't just an academic exercise. We had less than half the time that we had planned for our interview, but she was calm and comforting—and it all started to go smoothly. Her husband and her dog greeted me, and then her husband retired to the kitchen to get the supper and her dog soothed me by requiring to be stroked.

We prayed for a moment, and then I asked her if she

had enjoyed her years of being single. 'Yes,' she told me. 'Quite early on, when I was in my thirties, I realised that I needed to be whole—and if possible to be whole as a single person. Because if you aren't whole as a single person then you won't be whole married.

'So I can remember a very important occasion when I asked the Lord to make me whole, even if I was to remain single. I never said to the Lord that I would be willing to remain single for ever. I never thought I would be and I didn't want to be. I was prepared to be single "for now", and that was how it was. It was he who promised to make me whole—and he did. And it gave me a lot of happiness.'

I wondered how Patsy would define a whole human being and what the qualities were. She thought for a moment. 'What is wholeness? Obviously we need other people. Being whole doesn't mean that you can be an individual on your own and not need others. But it does mean that you are able to be free from the sort of needs that would be debilitating. So you are free to enjoy other people. You are free to enjoy all the happy things that life offers. You will have times of loneliness and needs of one sort and another, but not in a way that's debilitating or destructive.'

'Did you notice a difference after you prayed that prayer?' I asked her. 'Oh, yes,' she said. 'It had taken me a number of years to get there, to get to the point of really accepting. Before that I often used to go to new places, conferences or whatever, looking for who might be a partner. I would sort of give everyone the once over to see if anyone was at all likely! And it wasn't helpful to live like that.

'Then I went through a difficult patch when I was very aware that everyone else seemed to have someone with them, or that they were pushing a pram, and that sort of thing. But after the Lord met me in this way—and it wasn't just praying a prayer, somehow it was a spiritual transaction, a sort of covenant—I knew it was all right. It didn't take away the desire for marriage, but being single was all right.'

I asked Patsy if she thought that single people who have managed to get it right and to be whole and complete in themselves have got a particular witness to make? 'Yes,' she said, 'I am sure they have. When I first had the opportunity to have a flat of my own as opposed to being in digs in someone else's home my worry wasn't so much about managing to get it set up. It was "Can you make a home as a single person."

'Round about that time I read Edith Schaeffer's book *Hidden Art*, and she was saying how you can make it home wherever you go. You take your little shell, or a photograph, or your cat. And when I was talking of that with a friend he said, "Yes, you need to be able to show that you can be single and have a home," and I believe that was right. There was no reason to think that because I was on my own I couldn't have a home. So I made the flat into a home, and it was a home.

'I was quite poor. My sister even had to lend me some money for a carpet, and I had to have the cheapest of everything. Friends were very helpful in lending me things, and some bought me things. One friend bought a fridge for me. And it wasn't a scrappy home. Somehow it was able to be nice. It was a flat, and there was a little balcony, and I grew tomatoes and morning glory up the side—and in that way it was homely.

'And I entertained people. I entertained some single people and I entertained couples, and I know they could see that being on your own didn't mean you were half. Being on your own you could be whole.

'Because I didn't have a lot of time I couldn't be as adventuresome as I've been able to be since I got married, but I think I have got a creative streak which really began to show itself when I had this home. That's when it began to show most. So that came out in my cooking, and I did try to have proper supper parties for couples now and again, as well as having lots of single people.

'At the time I was working among students, so I ran a Sunday tea. I used to get two of the students to make the cakes, and I had loads of students in and out on Sunday afternoon, as well as through the week. So I used the home for my work but I also used it for entertaining at all sorts of levels. Sometimes my godchildren came to stay, and I used to give them baked beans and the sort of things that children like.'

I asked Patsy if she had had a car, and if she had whether it was helpful. 'Very helpful,' she said. 'Imperative! One of the perks of being single was being able to have holidays. I always had a friend that I could go on holidays with over the eighteen years that I was in parish work. In fact I had a series of three different friends, one of whom was my sister. We always went abroad, and one of us having a car was such a help. And just getting away for a day off. You *must* be able to get a day off.'

Some women feel incomplete to go on holiday with a woman and not a man, and I wondered if Patsy did. 'No, not at all. In the earlier days a friend and I camped, and that was always fun. I hadn't travelled much before then, and going abroad was so stimulating and there was so much to see that I just enjoyed it all.'

'When things really hurt and were difficult,' I asked her, 'how did you pray?' She considered for a moment: 'I can't really remember. I know at one stage when I went to a wedding and found that very difficult I said to myself "I'm never going to a wedding again," which was the coward's way out, but I needed to escape for a while. So I didn't go to any for a bit, but then I began to be able to.

'Another time I went to stay with a friend who was newly married and expecting her first baby. That was very painful, and then I said, "I won't go and stay with a newly married friend again!" And for a while I didn't, although it just so happened that I wasn't invited, so that situation didn't occur again for a long time and then it seemed to be easier. But I don't know how I prayed. I somehow simply poured out to God how I felt.'

'So you were really open to God about all your feelings?' I questioned.

'Yes, I found I tended to be someone who could be more open with God than with people. I've had to learn to be more open with people. I can remember one time when I was very low about it all I was telling God that it wasn't fair, and this was in the middle of the night (these things usually are!), and what he seemed to tell me to do was to look up verses about seeking God in the night.

'I did look up all those references and that was very helpful, because the Psalmist looks for God in the night, and his tears are in the night, and God meets him in the night and promises his beloved sleep in the night. I found comfort in that.

'So yes, I did try to tell God just how I felt. Sometimes I would pray in tongues, and that would be very helpful.'

I asked her whether she had ever found that married couples were tactless in the way they spoke to her. She said 'I could certainly relate to the bit you've started your book with: "You're such a nice girl, why aren't you married?" But it didn't seem to happen so much latterly. More when I was a bit younger—or that's when I remember it, and perhaps that's why it hurt more.

'I think I have been saved some of the pain of some of my single friends because of the status my job gives me in the church. Because of that people are happy to invite me to a meal. But I can remember one friend who had been in her church for about twenty years who could still count on one hand the couples who had invited her on her own, and that was very hurtful.

'I remember going out once with a couple who had been married a long time and had four children. I sat in the back of their car with the two of them in the front, and then when we were walking through the woods they held hands. I said to myself, "If ever I get married (and it was still many years away) then I shall always try to put the single one, the third one, in the front." And however much I loved my partner I wouldn't hold hands when there were three of us. But this couple had no idea they were being hurtful.

'I have been fortunate in being single because I have had good friends all along the way. I do feel for the friends who are single who can't think of someone to go on holidays with, or what to do on a day off. That's really hard, and I don't know why it happens.'

'But some people just aren't good at making friends,' I commented. 'And there are some people who say, "If only I had a friend," and they try to latch on to you. I think they need to learn how to make friends. What sort of qualities do you think you need to be a friend?'

'Well, you've got to be able to give,' Patsy answered. 'I suppose it comes down to this wholeness again. Some of the people without friends are very "Poor me" for one reason or another. And you *have* to be outgoing, which is the same for marriage, and why I think this wholeness goes right the way through. You have to be free from yourself. Perhaps a definition of wholeness is "being free from yourself".

'Being single I can't tell you how much having a dog made a difference. The companionship of this animal (at this point Patsy stroked the ears of the lovely black dog, Rory, who was leaning against her knee) when I came in in the evening, or at any time of day—and the wag of the tail, and being able to stroke him, and being made to get out to take him for walks. This dog has been wonderful!'

'You can go over the top when you get fond of a dog,' I said. 'Were you ever tempted to?'

'I was aware of the dangers. You notice it with married people sometimes, when they are for ever talking about their babies. And you can go over the top talking about your animal. So I was aware of it. But I don't think I fell into the trap. I hope I didn't. He's a naughty dog and he does naughty, wicked things, so I got a reputation! But I don't think I talked about him more than he should have been talked about.

'Sometimes I had meetings in my house and he'd be in the room. As soon as we said the Grace then he'd get up, because he knew it was the end. And he would welcome people!

'When you have an animal, especially a dog, you have got to be in an area where you can walk him. That's vital, so that he's not just cooped up in a flat all day. The other thing is that you need a back stop to look after him. You must have your holidays, and dogs can't always go on holiday with you if you are going abroad. So you need someone to look after them.

'I had some dog-loving friends plus my sister, and he has a range of three or four people he can go to. They love him to come and stay. Now I didn't know about that in advance, but it had been prayed about a lot—whether I should have him, or have a dog at all, and which was the right dog for me and would be the right parish dog. And then I was even provided with homes for him when I was away.'

I asked Patsy if there was anything she wanted to say that I hadn't asked her about, and she looked thoughtful for a moment. Then she said: 'One of the verses that has helped me all along is "I know the plans I have for you, says the Lord, plans for welfare and not for evil, to give you a future and a hope" (Jer 29:11) I always believed that would apply to marriage, although I didn't have any evidence of it.

'And that verse in Hebrews 12:11, that 'For the moment all discipline seems painful rather than pleasant', but afterwards the opposite, that sometimes came to me when I was going through a difficult patch, that it does 'yield the peaceful fruit of righteousness.' And I believed that.

'I believe that God does know best. Although I waited until I was in my mid-forties to get married I don't think that God has made a mistake. Had I gone on being single, if that had been his way, then that wouldn't have been a mistake either. He is to be trusted—and where he's put us he can make us whole.'

NOTES

1. Shirley Conran *Superwoman* (First published Sidgwick & Jackson; London, 1975; Penguin Books 1977).
2. Sebastian Moore. Taken from *The Inner Loneliness* (Darton, Longman and Todd Ltd, 1982).
3. Bishop Fulton Sheen *The Power of Love* (Maco Corporation Inc, 1964; Peter Davies, London, 1966).
4. Christopher Bryan *Nightfall* (Lion, Tring, 1986).
5. Fynn *Mister God This is Anna* (Collins, London, 1974; Fount, London 1977).
6. Julian of Norwich *Revelations of Divine Love* (Fifteenth century).

2

God's Plan and Purpose For Us

Most of us grow up assuming that one day we shall be married. We are brought up to believe that the road from girlhood to womanhood and happiness will run at some point up the aisle of a church. We shall walk up the aisle, wearing white, on our father's arm, and then be handed over to the bridegroom of our choice who is standing there waiting for us.

Probably we will start to readjust our ideas in our mid-twenties or early thirties, because it is really only then that we begin seriously to think that perhaps Mr Right isn't going to turn up after all.

In order to make the readjustment successfully we need to take a long clear look at what we want out of life. In most cases I think that a girl who desperately wants to get married can and will do so, because she will be more concerned about just being married than she will about the sort of man she marries.

But for the rest of us a much more crucial question is what sort of husband we want, which we cannot separate from the most important thing of all—what we believe the will of God is for our own life.

I took part once in a teach-in on sex in a young people's group attached to a church. One of the questions asked by a man (anonymously!) was read out by the chairman: 'I can't seem to find a girl who is both spiritual and sexy: why?' I cannot remember how we answered his question—which sent a wave of laughter rippling all round the hall. What I do remember is being delighted that I had raised the problem earlier in the evening from the woman's point of view. 'The sort of man who was both spiritual and masculine doesn't exactly grow on trees!' I had said. A lot of Christian women make exactly the same complaint, and say that the Christian men they know are 'wet', or 'wimps'.

My own youthful daydream of a perfect Christian husband was a man with a spirituality like St Paul's, a delight in sex like the man in the Song of Solomon (which could hardly be discovered in its totality or even perhaps developed until after marriage, so I was dreaming an impossible dream), a delicious sense of humour, and a deep understanding of how human beings can help one another to grow towards wholeness. But to ask for all that and to refuse to settle for anything less is to be like a child who cries for the moon to play with and then sulks when she can't have it.

We all know that we have to make a compromise between the qualities we would like in a partner and the reality of things as they are. When two people love each other then they can change and grow and develop qualities that they didn't have before. But we can only compromise so far, and if we do not meet someone we can really love then it is no use marrying someone whom we don't love.

But there is another problem. There are far more Christian single women around than there are heterosexual single Christian men. The obvious solution to the problem would seem to be that we should marry non-Christian men—but the New Testament says that is a spiritual impossibility (however legally possible it might be).

In 2 Corinthians 6:14 it says that the yoking together

of a Christian with a non-Christian is like trying to join light to darkness, or Christ to Satan. The Christian wife is not just the same sort of person as her non-Christian husband with an extra bit tacked on which is her Christianity. She is a totally 'new creature', and she belongs to the 'new creation'. The husband doesn't share this life at all, and is spiritually 'dead'. The essentially different and spiritual quality of *her* life is the relationship which she has with Christ, which is what eternal life is. If her husband doesn't have a similar relationship there will be a deep division between them. They will not share in the most important relationship of all—and the woman will find herself in a terrible conflict of loyalties.

It is no use marrying a non-Christian husband with a view to getting him 'converted' afterwards. Women who have done so have found from bitter experience that it simply doesn't work out like that. Although they are still Christians they find it almost impossible to make any progress in their spiritual life. Worst of all, they are grieving the Spirit of God who dwells within them.

But what are we to do if we believe that we shouldn't marry non-Christians, yet either there are no Christian candidates at all or else the ones that do present themselves simply don't appeal to us? This was one of the problems that faced Aredi, because as the daughter of a Greek father she could have had a marriage arranged for her. When she got to the age to be married her parents said, 'We'll introduce you to some nice Greek boys.' They produced quite a few of them, and in two cases things could have developed. But at that point Aredi had become a Christian, and this wasn't what she wanted.

Yet it is perplexing. Her human father would have arranged a marriage for her. But her heavenly Father hasn't. The Bible says that God will guide us every step of the way through our lives, and that he will fulfill his purpose for us and in us.

But it says in Genesis that God made woman to be 'a

helpmeet for man'. If his original purpose in creating us was that we should be wives, how can he be said to have fulfilled his purpose for us if he doesn't provide us with husbands? It is as if a boat builder made a boat and left it permanently in the boat yard. He never launched it to sail on the water, and so it never fulfilled the very purpose for which he apparently designed and made it.

There seem to be two answers to this dilemma. The first answer is that God didn't *just* design us to be wives and mothers. The Westminster Confession says that the *chief* end of man is to glorify God, and to enjoy him for ever. In the next chapter we shall look at what it might really mean that God created woman as a helper or a helpmeet for man. Because often we don't realise what a helper is in the plan and purpose of God.

The second answer to the question is given in what Jesus said about people making themselves eunuchs for the sake of the kingdom of heaven. Some are incapable of marriage from birth, some are made incapable by the action of men, and some have made themselves so for the sake of the Kingdom of Heaven (Mt 19:12 J B Phillips).

I believe that a woman who narrows her choice of a husband to men who are Christians, and who rejects the possibility of marriage to a non-Christian (because such a marriage is not the will of God), really can be said to have made herself 'incapable of marriage for the sake of the kingdom of heaven.'

Those of us who are not married need to have a vision of what the single life is meant to be in the plan and purpose of God. It says in the book of Haggai that 'where there is no vision the people perish,' and there is a real sense in which we shall perish as single people if we do not have a true vision. We live in a world which sees a false vision, with an unreal, idealised colour TV picture of a smiling husband, a smiling wife and two smiling children as the model of real happiness. But the world is not seeing straight, and it is sad to say that very often the church doesn't see straight either.

Many single people find themselves undervalued and unappreciated in the churches. The family service is often the normal Sunday service, and single people are seen as oddities and misfits. I was very displeased when a woman came up to me once in a local church and said, 'I saw you were on your own, so I've come to speak to you,' with a monumental tactlessness, placing me immediately in the category of those people who need to be Done Good To—and making me want to say ungraciously, 'Well if that's your only reason you needn't have bothered.'

A few months ago I sat next to two women in another church, which I had just started to go to. While we were waiting for the service to begin one of them said, 'Hullo' and gave me a warm welcome. Then she started to apologise that there weren't many people there (although there were nearly a hundred, and most vicars would be falling over themselves with joy to have that many at Evensong). 'Nearly everyone has gone to the Parish Weekend,' she explained. 'That's nice,' I said. 'Why didn't you go?'

Her answer horrified me. 'Well, it's really for families and couples.' I told her that was outrageous and that it ought to be changed. By then her friend had joined in the conversation and they suggested that next year those of us who were single could back one another up and go in a group.

The vicar and many of the families in that church would have been just as horrified as I was that that woman felt as she did. But the fact remains that she felt like it because of the way the church was run and the families in it behaved.

Married people are often blind to the qualities of single people, and they need to ask Christ to heal their blindness. But single people can be just as blind, and there is a particular condition of blindness that affects the single woman.

It is a painful condition, because it has to do with the fundamental question that we have been looking at in this chapter. Are we somehow falling short of God's original and best purpose for woman? We keep asking deep, searching and painful questions about what that purpose really is. And since the only way really to get the answers right is to do some theology and some Bible study, that is what we shall do in the next chapter.

3

The Theology of the Single Life

The problem about the theology of the single life starts right back at the beginning, in the book of Genesis. Or at least, it does for those of us who take the Bible at all seriously—and if we don't then it won't be Christian theology that we are studying, but some other sort.

In that most beautiful telling of the mystery of the creation it says that after God had made the world and all its creatures he made a creature who was different. This creature was still made of the same material as the other creatures—out of the dust of the earth—but in the image and likeness of God, and with the breath of God breathed into his nostrils to make him a living creature unique among all the rest.

Yet the image and likeness of God wasn't to be made known by just one creature. It was to be made known by two.

> So God created man in his own image, in the image of God he created him; male and female he created them (1:27).

But then there is another telling of what went on in the mind of God when he made the special creature who was like himself, so therefore male *and* female.

Then the Lord God said, 'It is not good that the man should be alone; I will make him a helper fit for him' (2:18).

For the single woman (and perhaps for all women) this is where the problem and the questions start. Did God create women just to help men and stop them being lonely?

If the answer to that question is 'yes' then it is difficult to see how those of us who are single are fulfilling the purpose of God, unless the job that you do or that I do happens to help a man to do *his* job better.

I once went on an unusual working holiday with three clergymen. We stayed in a farmhouse at the top of a high cliff overlooking the sea, the smell of gorse filled the air and seabirds wheeled and screamed overhead. I slept and worked in the farmhouse, and each of the men slept and worked in one of three outbuildings set up as study bedrooms. Their work was to write books. Mine was to cook, and produce delicious meals (to help and encourage their writing) at the proper times. One of them wrote a book within the week. The other two struggled and hardly wrote anything.

The spirit that was struggling within me, with those cries and sighs that are 'too deep for words' made itself known in a feeling (uncertain and very unsure of itself) that it was I who had the gift of writing, and not the two who found it so hard. Both of them had been supremely gifted to preach (the third man could preach *and* write), one of them with a unique ability.

The gift and the spirit that stirred and struggled within me to express itself in writing was a higher gift than cooking and looking after men, and until it was born I could never be satisfied—and nor could the Spirit who gave me the gift. I am not a great writer and I never shall be. Just a very ordinary one. But I seem to be able to write about God and about Christianity in a way that ordinary people can understand—and if that is the gift that the Spirit has chosen to give me then I must use it.

That all happened back in the sixties. Yet the belief that women's sole purpose in life is to help men and stop them being lonely is still around, and it stems from that verse in Genesis which I quoted above:

> It is not good that the man should be alone: I will make an help meet for him, or (RSV) I will make him a helper fit for him.

The feminist movement says that it isn't true that woman's purpose in life is to help man, but some of us shout so loudly that I suspect we are trying to drown the voice inside us that says it is. Others of us can say quite softly that it is not our only purpose to help men, because we do not want to believe the inner conviction which tells us it is what God is saying. The only way to be sure what that voice says is to listen to the Word of God and find out what it really is saying and what it means.

It is a fascinating study to look up the word help in a concordance. The first time the Hebrew word *ezer* (help) is used is in the Genesis passage we have been looking at: the concept of the help or helper is introduced in 2:18, and again in 2:20 we hear there was not found a helper fit for him among either the birds of the air or the beasts of the field. Almost all the other times the words is used it refers to God.

> The God of my father was my help, and delivered me from the sword of Pharaoh (Ex 18:4);
>
> There is none like God, O Jeshurun, who rides through the heavens to your help, and in his majesty through the skies (Dt 33:26);
>
> Our soul waits for the Lord; he is our help and shield (Ps 33:20);
>
> But I am poor and needy; hasten to me, O God! Thou art my help and my deliverer; O Lord, do not tarry! (Ps 70:5);

I have laid help upon one who is mighty (Ps 89:19 AV);

Our help is in the name of the Lord, who made heaven and earth (Ps 124:8).

There are more than a dozen other references to the fact that it is the Lord who is the help (or helper) of his people. So if we are really going to listen to what the Word of God says about what it means to be a help or a helper perhaps we shall have to change our minds and revise our opinions.

Most of us think of a help as someone who is inferior. 'He's just the hired help,' people say (or she is) and the fact that they know they really ought not to talk like that isn't the point. The point is that in the Bible a helper isn't someone who is inferior and who does the dirty jobs—although the helper who is the true image of God will in fact do the dirty jobs, just as Jesus took the role of the servant and washed his disciples' feet, and turned the world's valuation of things on its head by telling us that whoever would be greatest among us must be our servant. We must look at what it means to be a servant in that sense.

Ruth Etchells told me once how powerfully and deeply that account in John's Gospel of Jesus washing the disciples' feet affected her—and how it was wonderfully effective in the healing of a difficult relationship.[1] When she became Principal of St John's College, Durham she found herself struggling with the problem of how to exercise authority in a way that was right.

A situation had brewed up in which she could well have to confront a man on the college staff about something he was doing. In the middle of this situation, when she was turning it all over in her mind and feeling troubled, she found herself reading John 13:3–5: 'Jesus knew that the Father had put all things under his power and that he had come from God.' At that moment in his consciousness there was a climax of absoluteness of power and authority—a far greater power and authority than any of us can ever have or know. And at that very moment, with that awareness and knowledge, he took a towel, wrapped it round his waist like an apron, and then poured water into a basin and started to wash his disciples' feet. It was a dirty, lowly job, and he did it with love—and then challenged them to go and do the same thing.

> Do you understand what I have done for you? You call me 'Teacher' and 'Lord', and rightly so, for that is what I am. Now that I, your Lord and Teacher, have washed your feet, you also should wash one another's feet. I have set you, an example, that you should do as I have done for you (Jn 12–15).

Then Ruth Etchells felt an enormous sense of relief. She wasn't being asked to say that there shouldn't be authority, whoever it was vested in—teachers or judges or bishops. Those were proper roles for humanity. But the passage was saying that Christians had to find a way to wash the feet of the people among whom they exercised their authority and whom they lived with and worked with.

Ruth had a proper authority given to her as the Principal of St John's, and the man who was being difficult was under her authority. But she had to exercise that authority over him as a servant. When the man came in to see her she shared her understanding of that incident in the life of Jesus. Then she asked him a question. 'Please, will you tell me—how can I kneel and wash your feet?' At that point their encounter broke right open. The man had come in prepared for battle and expecting a telling off. Yet they both found themselves at the feet of Christ, asking 'Please, will you help us to sort this one out?'

When we act as servants in the right way we are showing forth God in the world and in the church, which has not paid anything like the attention it should have done to what Jesus said about serving:

You know that the rulers of the Gentiles lord it over them, and their great men exercise authority over them. It shall not be so among you; but whoever would be great among you must be your servant, and whoever would be first among you must be your slave; even as the Son of man came not to be served but to serve, and to give his life as a ransom for many (Mt 20:25–28).

There is a lovely hymn which expresses this perfectly called 'The servant king':

> From heaven you came,
> Helpless babe,
> Entered our world,
> Your glory veiled;
> Not to be served
> But to serve,
> And to give your life,
> That we might live.
>
> This is our God,
> The Servant King,
> He calls us now
> To follow him,
> To bring our lives
> As a daily offering
> Of worship to
> The Servant King.[2]

When we look at Jesus as the servant we get a particular understanding of what God is like. But the servant is not the same as the helper, even though sometimes the roles merge into one.

The helper gives us another insight into the nature of God, and since it says that the helper is especially what woman is (in God's creation of the human race in his image and likeness) we must go on looking at God as the helper of his people.

The divine helper is the one who helps his people when they cannot manage on their own. Often what happens is that when they get in a mess they cry out to God to come and help them and (if possible) to hurry up and do it quickly. But that is not how it is really meant to be. When we get it right we know that we need help all the time. It isn't that we can manage some parts of our life by ourself and just need God's help for the difficult bits—like a schoolgirl who can manage the arithmetic homework but asks her father for help with the algebra. The truth of the matter is that 'Without me you can do nothing'.

The Christian life is a life that is lived *in union* with God. 'I live, yet not I, but Christ liveth in me' (Gal 2:20). On our own we cannot even pray right. But 'the Spirit helps us in our weakness; for we do not know how to pray as we ought, but the Spirit himself intercedes for us with sighs too deep for words' (Rom 8:26).

It is vitally important for a woman's sense of worth to realise that when God created her to be a 'help' for man she was created in the image and likeness of the Lord who is the supreme helper.

That is not to say that only women are helpers and that men are not. That would be an absurd way to understand Scripture. But I wanted us to look at what it means to be a helper so that we get it firmly into our heads that to be a *helper* is not an inferior role. Anything but. And to realise this is to be on the way to being transformed by the renewing of our minds.

Genesis is saying that it is man and woman together who are made in the image and likeness of God. The church Fathers didn't see it that way. 'The woman together with her own husband is the image of God,' wrote Augustine, 'so that the whole substance may be one image; but when she is referred to separately in her quality of helpmate, which regards the woman herself alone, then she is not the image of God; but as regards the man alone, *he is the image of God as fully and completely as when the woman too is joined to him*' (my italics).

In the church law that comes down to us from that
time a man called Gratian, who was a jurist from
Bologna, goes even futher. 'Women should be subject to
their men. The natural order for mankind is that women
should serve men and children their parents, for it is just
that the lesser serve the greater. The image of God is in
man and it is one. Women were drawn from man, who
has God's jurisdiction as if he were God's vicar, because
he has the image of the one God. Therefore woman is not
made in God's image. Woman's authority is nil; let her
in all things be subject to the rule of man . . . And neither
can she teach, nor be a witness, nor give a guarantee, nor
sit in judgment. Adam was beguiled by Eve, not she by
him. It is right that he whom woman led into wrongdo-
ing should have her under his direction, so that he may
not fail a second time through female levity' (*Corpus Iuris
Canonici*).

The Fathers have had a powerful influence on the
church right down to the present day, and sometimes it
has been a bad influence. We need to look at what they
said in the light of the Word of God, and where it
contradicts the Word then we need to change our attitudes and help other people to change theirs. It is the
truth that will set us free. If we look at that last quotation
from Gratian we shall see how untrue it is. 'And neither
can she . . . be a witness.' But that is quite simply untrue
according to the New Testament, because women were
witnesses to the resurrection of Christ, and the Gospels
recognise their witness.

The way that Jesus treated women was quite different
to the way that the men of his day treated them—and
quite different from some men of our day! He had a deep
theological conversation with the woman of Samaria (Jn
4:7–42) and when his disciples came back with the food
they had gone to buy it says that 'they marvelled that he
was talking with a woman'. They were surprised because
to do such a thing in the street was simply not done. It
wasn't respectable.

It was surprising too that Jesus talked to the woman about theological issues, because women were never taught theology. All the prohibitions of the Jewish law applied to them, and it was only the men who ever studied the law and the prophets. There was no 'bar mitzvah' for a girl, and a woman could never be a proper Jew because she could not go through the initiation rite and be circumcised.

In Old Testament times women were only allowed to go a little way in to the Temple. They could go as far as the Court of the Women (beyond the 'middle wall of partition' or 'dividing wall of hostility' [Eph 2:14] which kept the Gentiles out). Only Jews (ie circumcised Jewish men) were allowed beyond that wall into the Court of Israel, which was raised a little above the Court of the Women. At the Feast of Tabernacles men could go into the innermost Court of the Priests, where the altar stood. But into the Holy of Holies only the high priest could go, and that only once a year on the Day of Atonement. He carried sacrificial blood to atone for the sins of the people into the holy place 'within the veil' where the presence of God dwelt.

The New Testament uses those images to show what happened when Christ died. He entered *once for all* into the Holy Place, taking not the blood of goats and calves but his own blood, thus securing an eternal redemption (Heb 9:12). And having gone within the veil (or into the inner shrine behind the curtain) he has become a high priest for ever after the order of Melchizedek (Heb 6:19, 20). We do not need priests any more (either male priests or women priests), because the way into the presence of God is permanently open.

The dividing wall of hostility that used to divide Jew from Gentile has been broken down in Christ. Since the death of Christ women no longer have to stay in the Court of the Women. Women as well as men can enter now into the presence of God, into the holiest place of all, and Gentiles as well as Jews can enter.

> For as many of you as were baptized into Christ have
> put on Christ. There is neither Jew nor Greek, there is
> neither slave nor free, there is neither male nor female;
> for you are all one in Christ Jesus (Gal 3:27,28).

Paul is writing there about groups of people who had
been divided but between whom there had now been
reconciliation. Now they were all one in Christ Jesus. Yet
it takes a very long time to discover the riches and enter
into the freedom that we can have in Christ.

Daphne Wales, a prominent lay reader in the Church
of England, showed me something about that marvellous
statement of Paul that I had never seen before. She said
that it happened quite early that Jews and Gentiles
found themselves reconciled in Christ (which is not to
say that all of them were, or that the way that some so-
called Christians have treated Jews in the past is anything but a scandalous offence to the name of Christ, and
a cause for deep shame and penitence in the church that
bears his name).

Then hundreds of years passed before the implications
started to be worked out of slaves and free people being
one in Christ Jesus. And it is only in recent years that the
issue of male and female in Christ has begun to be looked
at and worked on.

NOTES

1. Shelagh Brown *Lent for Busy People* (BRF, London, 1987), p
   105.
2. From *The Servant King* by Graham Kendrick, copyright
   © Make Way Music, administered by Thankyou Music,
   PO Box 75, Eastbourne, BN23 6NW.

4

How Can I Be Fulfilled?

The most heart-searching question of all that we can ever ask ourselves as single women is whether we can really be fulfilled people if we are not married. My answer to that question is a passionate, heartfelt Yes, because there has only ever been one totally fulfilled human being in the whole world—and he was single.

Jesus achieved his rich humanity without entering into the deeply personal relationship that marriage is meant to be. But he didn't achieve it without suffering:

> It was fitting that God, for whom and through whom everything exists, should, in bringing many sons to glory, make perfect through suffering the leader of their salvation (Heb 2:10).

The words 'make perfect' there mean to bring to fulfillment that which Jesus would be and do for the salvation of the world. If the sinless Son of God had to suffer to reach *his* fulfillment, we can hardly imagine that we shall not have to suffer to reach ours.

But we shall have to *want* to be fulfilled—and we shall need to believe that it is possible and that it is the will of God. It is no use fretting our lives away thinking, 'How different life would be if I was married.' Because it might not be—unless *we* were different.

Obviously it would be different in some ways. There would be a man around the house to stop us being alone—but perhaps not give us a chance to be on our own. There would be a man to go on holidays with—but perhaps not to the place *we* wanted to go. There would be a man splashing happily away and singing in the bath—and perhaps leaving a ring of scum round it afterwards; and then cleaning his teeth and squeezing the toothpaste at the wrong end of the tube (the right end being where *we* squeeze it).

Someone said, 'Marriage doesn't solve any of your problems; if you're frustrated before you're married you'll still be frustrated afterwards,' and whether we are successful at being married or successful at being single will all depend on the sort of person we are.

I am a great admirer of John Powell's books, which I have found very helpful indeed in discovering how to be braver in loving other people. My three favourites are *Why Am I Afraid to Tell You Who I Am*; *Why Am I Afraid To Love*; and *Fully Human, Fully Alive*. The descriptions of John Powell that I have read, and people I have met who know him, say that that last title describes just how he is. A person who is fully human and fully alive. He is an outgoing, immensely loving human being, with an enormous capacity for self-giving and understanding.

But John Powell is a single man. He is a Roman Catholic priest, and therefore celibate.

He begins his book *Why Am I Afraid To Tell You Who I Am* with two quotations. One is from Genesis 2:18.

> Then the Lord God said: 'It is not good for man to be alone'.

The other is from Paul Tournier, on *Understanding the Human Condition*.

> How beautiful, how grand and liberating this
> experience is, when people learn to help each other. It is

> impossible to over-emphasise the immense need
> humans have to be really listened to, to be taken
> seriously, to be understood.
>
> Modern psychology has brought it very much to our
> attention. At the very heart of all psychotherapy is this
> type of relationship in which one can tell everything,
> just as a little child will tell all to his mother.
>
> No one can develop freely in this world and find a full
> life without feeling understood by at least one
> person. . . .
>
> He who would see himself clearly must open up to a
> confidant freely chosen and worthy of such trust . . .[1].

In an ideal world and in an ideal marriage a wife would
be her husband's confidant and he would be hers. But in
the world as it really is that doesn't always happen.

A single woman once spoke to me yearningly out of her
loneliness about a married woman whom we both knew:
'Look at her,' she said, 'She's got everything—a husband and a family and that enormous house, and they go
on those super holidays . . .'

What I couldn't tell the unmarried woman was of the
heartache and unhappiness of this married woman. She
and her husband never spoke of the things that really
mattered, and although she wasn't alone she felt desperately lonely.

But there is a way out of shallow relationships for
anyone who is prepared to take it, and it is one of the
ways towards maturity. It will also have a profound
effect on our own inner loneliness. I discovered it myself
when I was reading Dr Frank Lake's *Clinical Theology*.[2]
He wrote of the vital need for openness and of the way it
could affect all our relationships.

We need help from one another, and just as perfection-
ist attitudes disqualify us from being 'the kind of person
to whom broken people can come with an assurance of
acceptance in the power of Christ's acceptance, so the
same attitudes of obsessional need to be in the right, or of

a proud need to be thought by others to be as good as we seem to be, prevent many of us from coming for help when we most need it.'

Frank Lake continues 'Of all the difficulties encountered in clinical theological practice, pride in those who ought to be helped and prayerlessness (a crass form of pride) in those who ought to be helping, are perhaps the commonest and the most formidable. Nothing so breaks communion between God and man, and man and man, as pride and prayerlessness.

'Those who work in this field find that three things invariably accompany one another for good.

'First, openness towards God in a life of closer obedience, with that alert readiness which arises out of a persistent prayer life, so that common talk slips naturally into conversation about the ultimates of existence.

'Second, openness towards another [person] about one's own unresolved fears and lusts, rages and depressions, sins and unsuccessful struggles, an openness that may have been hellish hard to reach, over the conventional high walls of religious pride, breached only through prayer and obedience.

'Third, an openness towards others, which they can usually recognise before we can. Our own inner openness to God and to [another human being] to gain help for ourselves brings a new coin into circulation.

'We recognise that with the breakdown of existential distrust between ourselves and God, stemming from the breakthrough of confession to, or of an appeal for counsel from [another person] there has come into our lives a new and undeniable sense of being and well-being, a peace with God, with man, and with our own nature. This fulfills what we have always somehow known we were meant for. This is one side, our side, of the coin.

'The other side of the coin is recognised first by others. Is it what Sir Walter Scott called, in his mother, "innerliness"? Bishop Taylor Smith used to speak of peace as the side of the coin known to us, and power as the side manifest to others.'

Before this breakthrough happens in a person, very few other people will have come to ask for help. 'But now,' says Frank Lake, 'they come as if drawn by some irresistible attraction.'

To be open with God is to tell God all about ourself (or at least, all that we know)—our feelings, our hopes, our dreams, our fears, and our loves and our hates. In another place in the book Frank Lake gives some profound guidance about how to pray in that sort of way. Because when we open up to God like that what we are in fact doing is to pray.

Lake is actually writing about a depressed or afflicted person who 'has stopped praying because he cannot, or feels he cannot, turn either the depravities of rage and lust, or the deprivations of faithlessness, anxiety and emptiness into prayer'. But what he says is just as relevant to us, because that sort of praying is essential for everyone, and it is biblical:

> In *everything* by prayer and supplication, with thanksgiving, let your requests be made known unto God, and the peace of God, which passes all understanding, will keep your hearts and your minds in Christ Jesus (Phil 4:6–7).

Lake says that if a person has stopped praying because he doesn't feel he can pray about all the things in his life (and since in our case it will be in her life I am going to change the gender of the pronouns), then 'prayer as communication with God cannot be re-established unless she can bring her complaints, objections, demands, accusations, resentments, doubts and disbeliefs out of hiding, and into conversation with the pastor and with God. . . .

'The task of clinical pastoral care is to evoke the truth in the inward parts, however scandalous it may be, so as to bring the total actual content of the personality and its roots into the conversation with God—which is prayer' (p 40).

Perhaps the actual content of our personality may not be 'scandalous', but when we really get in touch with what is within us we are almost certain to discover pain, resentment and a certain amount of anger. They will be like wounds festering inside us, and they will go on hurting us until we let the Spirit of Christ uncover them and heal them.

But we still haven't gone all the way even when we have been totally open with God. The second stage is for us to be open with *one* other person. It cannot be such a profound openness as it is with God, but it can still be very deep—and if we are going to get the self-understanding that we need in order to grow to Christian maturity we shall have to do it.

As Tournier would put it, 'She who would see herself clearly must open up to a confidant freely chosen and worthy of such trust.'

For some people that confidant might be a minister or priest—but we had better be sure first of all that they are competent and second that they are trustworthy. If we simply assume that they are because of the job they do then we are being naive.

The person with whom I was totally open was a married Christian called Barbara, and I found myself astonished at what happened—in just the way that Frank Lake had said it would. Other people I know have had the same experience after being open first of all with God and then with another person. It is one of the ways to spiritual growth and maturity, and both of those things are essential if we are ever going to be fulfilled human beings.

As Christian single women we must take this matter of spiritual growth very seriously. A lot of Christians don't, and they are like the people to whom Paul wrote in Corinth:

> I was not able to talk to you as spiritual people; I had
> to talk to you as people still living by your natural
> inclinations, still infants in Christ; I fed you with milk
> and not solid food, for you were not yet able to take
> it. . . . (1 Cor 3:1,2 NJB).

Hebrews 5:11–14 says the same thing, and adds to it
that by now they ought to be mature:

> About this we have much to say which is hard to
> explain, since you have become dull of hearing. For
> though by this time you ought to be teachers, you need
> some one to teach you again the first principles of God's
> word. You need milk, not solid food; for every one who
> lives on milk is unskilled in the word of righteousness,
> for he is a child. But solid food is for the mature, for
> those who have had their faculties trained by practice to
> distinguish good from evil.

Immature Christians are like stunted plants, who have
never developed as they should have done. The way
market gardeners produce those short-stemmed chrysanthemums that we buy in pots is simply to deprive
them of light at a certain stage of growth. If they manage
to survive the winter (mine usually shrivel up unhappily)
and we plant them at the front of a flower border then we
discover our mistake, because when they get the proper
amount of light they grow up to their proper height of
two or three feet.

The poor chrysanthemums don't have a choice about
whether to grow or not. But we have a choice. We can be
feeble Christians, living in the half-light of compromise
and self-indulgence. Or we can walk in the light of Christ
and grow into the people that we are meant to be. Not
stunted human beings. But whole people, who are holy.

In the first chapter of this book I wrote, 'You are
God's work of art, and so am I: and to get it right we
have to work at it as well as God.' It is the same with
Christian maturity, which is almost a way of describing

what the work of art will be like when it is completed. There is God's side of it and our side of it. God's side of it is to work within us by the power of the Holy Spirit. Our side of it is to find out what Christian maturity is, and to discover how to grow.

NOTES

1. John Powell *Why Am I Afraid to Tell You Who I Am?* (Collins, London, 1975).
2. Frank Lake *Clinical Theology* (Darton, Longman & Todd, London, 1966).

5

Ways To Grow

The way we shall discover how to grow into the person God wants us to be is by going down the old, well-known paths of the Christian life. We shall tread the paths of prayer and worship, the paths of study and fellowship, and the path of service. We shall make new discoveries and see new things, or perhaps see old things in a new way, and it is the God of love who is calling us to grow and drawing us closer to himself in the process.

> With the drawing of this Love and the voice of this
> Calling
> We shall not cease from exploration
> And the end of all our exploring
> Will be to arrive where we started
> And know the place for the first time.[1]

But as we go along the well-known paths each one of us will discover different things on our walk or exploration, and each one of us will have a unique encounter with God and with all the people we shall meet along the way, because all of us are different, and each one of us is unique.

When I walk out of the back gate of my garden I step on to a path that runs between fields on either side and takes me up on to the Pilgrim's Way. But as I walk along that same path on different days it is a different walk.

Today I looked at the tiny, pale pink flowers that are just coming out on the blackthorn, and my heart was lifted up to God in a delighted, wordless wonder. It is Easter week, and the delicate flowers growing straight out of the black wood with its harsh thorns make me think of Christ on the cross. Just as there would be no flowers if there were no tree, so there would have been no shining Easter glory without the darkness of Good Friday.

But on another day it will be different. I shall walk up in quick, angry strides, and not notice any of the beauty around me. Then, perhaps, I shall have the experience of one of my favourite poems.

> He rode at furious speed to Broken Edge,
> And he was very angry, very small;
> But God was kind, knowing he needed not
> A scolding, nor a swift unpleasant fall,
> Nor any high reproach of soul at all.
> 'It matters not,' said Reason and Good Sense;
> 'Absurd to let a trifle grow immense.'
> 'It matters very much,' said Busy Brain;
> 'You cannot be content and calm again,
> For you are angry in a righteous cause.'
> 'Poor, queer old Waxy!' laughed the hips and haws,
> 'God has a sense of humour,' said a ball
> Of orange-gold inside a spindle-berry—
> 'And "Christ our Lorde is full exceeding merrie." '
> He lingered in the lane at Broken Edge,
> Bryony berries burned from every hedge;
> Snails in the deep wet grass of fairy rings
> Told him of unimaginable things.
> Love was in all the colours of the sky,
> Love in the folded shadows of the high
> Blue hills, as quiet as any Easter Eve.
> (O fool, O blind and earthbound thus to grieve!)

He turned his horse. Through level sunset-gleams
He saw a sudden little road that curled
And climbed elusive to a sky of dreams,
His anger over Broken Edge was hurled
To scatter into nothing on a gust
Of wind which brought the twilight to the trees.
The drifted leaves, the white October dust
Hiding the beechnuts for the squirrels' store,
Heard the low whisper spoken on his knees:—
'God, You have made a very perfect world,
Don't let me spoil it ever any more.'
(*Temper in October*, by V L Edminson)[2]

Nature itself is one of the ways through to God. Every created thing can show us its creator, if we look at it in the right way. And that is to have an inner awareness that God made it and also to have our eyes wide open and to pay deep attention as we look.

One way to meditate is to find something that is small enough to hold in the palm of our hand and to spend time looking at it, touching it, being aware of it, and letting it have all our attention. Perhaps a daisy, a conker, a leaf or a pebble. Or we could simply pay attention to one of our hands.

Another way to meditate is to sit quite still in a chair with our back straight, our knees and feet together, and our hands resting gently on our legs. Then we can take some deep breaths, letting our tension go away as we breathe out, and asking the Spirit of Christ to fill our hearts as we breathe in. After that, we can simply pay attention to every part of our body, starting with the top of our head and going right down to the tips of our ten toes.

The reason why that sort of meditation will be a way through to God for us is that the moment in which we meet God is always the present moment, and our bodies exist in the present moment. When I first used that particular meditation I found it had the extraordinary effect of making me start to cry, very gently.

Francis of Assisi used to call his body Brother Ass, and I suddenly became aware that my body was like a humble, patient donkey that I had simply taken for granted. Sister Donkey had done all that I had ever asked it to, but it wanted to be loved by its owner. As a child my mother had always been critical of my legs, and she had nick-named me 'Bandy', unaware of the awful pain I felt every time she said it—and how much I began to hate my ugly legs.

Yet after doing that meditation just once I began to feel a real affection for my legs, and I felt deeply grateful to them for the way they take me wherever I want to go. I ended up by just putting my hands on them and accepting them and saying I was sorry. In fact my legs are not ugly at all. They are quite good, and I have even had compliments about them! But I never believed the compliments, because they *felt* ugly, and because they did the whole of me felt ugly and inferior.

Another way to meet God in the present is to practise what Pierre de Caussade calls 'the sacrament of the present moment.' A sacrament is 'an outward and visible sign of an inward, invisible grace', so whatever happens to us in the present moment, and whatever we see and whoever we meet, is the visible thing through which the invisible God will make himself known to us within our hearts.

It is easy and entirely delightful to practise the sacrament of the present moment if we are looking at the tiny shining spheres of soap bubbles in the sink, or looking into the face of a friend who is smiling at us and loving us. It is much more difficult and not at all delightful when we are looking at a dead cat thrown on to the side of the road with its fur stiff with blood, or when another person has hurt us very deeply and we are feeling the pain of rejection.

Yet the painful things can be the sacrament of the presence of God just as much as the others. We can be

aware of Christ within us who said that not even a
sparrow fell to the ground without the presence of the
Father being there. We can be aware that one day the
whole creation will be freed from its slavery to corruption
and brought into the same glorious freedom as the children of God (Rom 8:21). We can be aware that Christ
knows what it is like to be despised and rejected of men,
and that in all our suffering he suffers with us.

Pierre de Caussade wrote that book when he was
spiritual director to a convent of nuns, and he was
exceedingly tough with them. When life was hard, he
said, they ought to be pleased, because it meant God was
teaching them even more important and difficult lessons,
and that was a cause for rejoicing and not complaining.

If we can find a good spiritual director we shall find
that this is another way to grow spiritually. A long time
ago I entirely disapproved of the idea. The Holy Spirit
was my director, and that was that. I had no intention of
letting somebody else tell me what to do, because God
would tell me.

But I simply had not realised how spiritual direction
works. I went to a director first of all because I was
envious of what another friend told me about hers—and
when I say that what I felt was envy I am giving the
word its meaning of 'A longing for another's advantages.'
So I wrote to her director, Fr Christopher Bryant, and
asked whether he would be willing to see me with a
possibility of taking me on. He said 'yes,' and then I
discovered all the advantages of spiritual direction for
myself.

What happened was that Christopher Bryant listened
to me. I talked about the things that were in my heart—
my joys, my sorrows, and all the things that God and I
were going to do with my life. I knew that everything I
said was in total confidence, so I felt safe. His part was to
comment on what I brought to him, and his skill was
such that I found myself understanding everything more

deeply, and growing into a deeper relationship with God. He prayed for me when I was there (and also, I know, when I wasn't there), and he suggested books for me to read. Never more than one at a time—but they were always profoundly helpful.

I only saw Christopher Bryant a few times before he died, but the hours we spent together were helpful beyond believing. This whole area of spiritual direction is a great lack in some sections of the church, and I am thinking very seriously about how that could be remedied. If you happen to feel the same, perhaps you would write to me (c/o Southwark Cathedral, London) and we can take it from there.

My spiritual director now is a woman—Sister Joan Harrow, of The Cenacle Retreat House at Hindhead (the place where Ruth Fowke goes for her retreats). Joan has directed me into an even deeper relationship with God. As the process has gone on I have found a new freedom from the chains of the past, chains that had shackled me and affected my behaviour and my actions. They were bound to. You cannot really dance for joy when you are in chains. You are afflicted by a certain limitation of movement and the sound of heavy clanking as you drag your past along with you.

Another thing that has happened under Joan's direction is that I have discovered what my strengths are, and then learned to work from those rather than struggle too much over my weaknesses. This came about through the Myers-Briggs Type Indicator. Joan gave me the initial assessment test as the introduction to an Ignatian retreat, and once we had discovered my type through taking a simple, half hour test, it showed me how I function in life. It was not at all arduous, and I wrote the answers to the questions sitting on a bench in the paved garden of The Cenacle with a cup of coffee on the arm of the seat and the birds singing in the trees.

I am what is known as an ENTJ—an Extraverted-

Intuitive-Thinking-Judging person. All those words have their special meanings. For example, Judging doesn't mean that I go round pointing a critical finger at everybody; it means that I use the judgement process of Thinking to deal with my outer world. If I had been an ENTP (or Perceptive) person it would have meant that I used the perceptive process of Intuition in dealing with my outer world.

But this is not the place to go into the theory of Myers-Briggs. I am mentioning it because it is a very useful tool for almost every area of life: how to get on with people and how to understand them—our families and our friends and the people we work with. It is relevant to the work that we do (or perhaps ought to be doing and aren't, because we have somehow got stuck in something that our personality type isn't very good at). It is also relevant to our prayer life and our spiritual development, because different prayer forms suit different personality types.

In *Prayer and Temperament*, by Chester P Michael and Marie C Norrisey[3], these are some of the things it says about the sort of prayer and worship which is most helpful to the ENTJ type which is mine:

> ENTJ's need good experience of community at liturgy and prefer congregational singing to other forms of . . . liturgy. They enjoy leading others in prayer and presiding at liturgies and prayer services. They love to be with people and therefore thoroughly enjoy celebrations "in the park". ENTJ's are often attracted to charismatic prayer groups and to singing the praises of God together . . .
>
> They need to develop regular habits of praying alone. It is strongly suggested that the ENTJ spend a few minutes at the beginning of each day using Centering Prayer to focus attention upon God and God's will for the events of the day. This could be repeated occasionally during the day and again in the evening before retiring . . .

If the Lectio Divina method is used, then approximately half the time should be spent on the second part of the exercise, the Meditation and Reflection on the insight received during the spiritual reading. (The facility of the ENTJ to solve complex problems, address complex issues, and come up with creative new ideas can be put to good use during this portion of private prayer) . . .

At the end of the prayer period the ENTJ should try to rest for a few minutes in the Lord's presence and wait quietly to see if any new thought or insight comes to mind. Quiet contemplation is needed by the workaholic, all-too-busy ENTJ.

How right that is! One of the other things that has to be done once we know the type we are is to recognise and develop the potential of our 'shadow', or undeveloped side. Some of the shadow qualities that I should consider at prayer, ponder upon, and act upon, are in these suggestions:

- Develop your own feelings; show warmth and express feelings to others.
- Be very considerate of the feelings of everyone you meet in the course of the day.
- Take time to listen to the point of view of others.
- Be open minded, flexible, adaptable.
- Be tolerant of the mistakes, limitations, failures of others.
- Without any previous planning, just take off for the day and do whatever your impulses lead you to do, as long as the actions would not be sinful.

There are other suggestions and directions for other types of people, but I have set out the ones for my type so that you can see how practical and wide ranging they are, and also how deeply spiritual. At the end of this chapter I have given a list of places where you could go to do a Myers-Briggs course. I did it on my own, but it is usually done in a group at a residential weekend.

The point of doing all this work on ourselves is so that we can live more effectively for God in the world that he made and loves and desires to save—and also to have a deeper, richer relationship both with God and with other people.

People love to be loved, and it is our inner fears that stop us loving. 'Perfect love casts out fear,' it says, but one of the ways he does it is to work gently and slowly within us so that all the fears that imprison us are cast out into the darkness—so that we can then walk out into the freedom of the light. But he will use other people to help us in that process.

Over the last six months I have been going to a Gestalt therapist. I never thought I would need to go to a therapist, because I imagined that therapists were only for people who were suffering from some sort of mental illness. It was a friend who suggested that I went. She had found it a help, and thought I would. She thought I had a potential for loving that had not yet come to its fruition, and because of what this therapist had done for her in that area she hoped the same thing might happen for me—and I think it is happening.

In the process of my therapy I have found a new freedom, a profound joy, and a deep peace. I only went a dozen times, and it seems that I do not need to go any more. But in working with a skilled therapist things in my past life that were unresolved were brought to a satisfactory conclusion. I could lay them peacefully and happily to rest—not with any ill will towards them, but with love. My mother who loved me but couldn't let me go. My father who loved me and thought I always had to be looked after and taken care of. My own inability to go away and leave them, because of what they told me would happen if I did. Other things, too, and other relationships.

The word 'Gestalt' means to complete, and now that all those things are completed and laid to rest my energy isn't with them in the past. It's all available for living in the present. I cannot explain why, but I know with a deeper certainty than I have before the truth that 'Nothing shall separate us from the love of God.'

> Thus was I learned that Love is our Lord's meaning. And I saw full surely in this, and in all, that ere God made us He loved us; which Love was never slaked, nor ever shall be. And in this Love He hath done all His works. And in this Love He hath made all things profitable to us. And in this Love our life is everlasting.
>
> (*Julian of Norwich*)

NOTES

1. T S Eliot 'Little Gidding' from *Four Quartets* (Faber & Faber, London).
2. V L Edminson 'Temper in October (ie Broken Edge)' from *Poems of Today* (Sidgwick & Jackson, London, 1935).
3. Chester P Michael and Marie C Norrisey *Prayer and Temperament: Different Prayer Forms for Different Personality Types* (The Open Door Inc, PO Box 855, Charlottesville, Virgina 22902, USA, 1984). By kind permission of Chester P Michael.

Places for Myers-Briggs Courses: The Cenacle, Grayshott, Hindhead, Surrey, GU26 6DN. Phone 042-873-4412. Emmaus House, Clifton Hill, Bristol, BS8 4PD. Phone 0272-738-056.

6

Homes, Homemaking and Entertaining

Nearly all the single women I know who have their own home say how much it means to them and what a difference it makes. I feel just the same. It was quite different to live in my home rather than my parents' home, and it somehow helped me to become my own person. It was my place, and I decorated it in my way, and I could entertain my friends in it whenever I wanted to. In fact I had lived alone in my parents' home for two years after first my mother and then my father had died. But it still felt quite different to move away from there and choose where I wanted to live.

I bought my present home sixteen years ago for £11,750. It is a small, semi-detached Edwardian house— a miner's cottage, going back to the days when they dug hearthstone out of the local hills. It looks up to the hills, and when I walk out of my back garden the path goes through fields straight up on to the Pilgrim's Way.

I love living here, and in spite of the way my house is going up in value I think I am very unlikely to move. It is worth £150,000 now, and increasing at the rate of £3,000 a month because it is only five minutes away from the M25. That may be an extreme example of the absurd thing that has happened to house prices over the last few years, but all of them have risen enormously.

This fact highlights the problem that faces anyone who wants to get her toe into the property market for the first time, unless she happens to be very rich. Most Christian single women are not.

But we have all got to live somewhere, so what are we to do? Some of us may live with our parents, but unless we are the only child and they leave us their house we shall then have to face the problem of finding our own home when prices have gone up even more.

We could find a cheap house if we decided to move to the North East (or if we live there already), but then we might not be able to get a job. Anyway, if we already have a circle of friends where we live now, we shall not want to move. Yet the situation is getting more serious as the months go by and house prices continue to rise.

One solution may be always to live in rented accommodation. But the price of that is going up all the time as well, and the money we are paying out on rent would probably be better spent on buying a place of our own. One bed sitting room in my area costs £40 per week at the moment. That probably includes a kettle, a tiny cooker, use of the bathroom, but no food. In the previous year the same thing cost £35 a week. It may be that some single women will choose to live like that and believe that it is how God means them to live. It will be to do with travelling light and following in the footsteps of Jesus, who said that 'the Son of Man has no place to lay his head.' But in one sense that was only literally true for three years. Up until then he had probably lived at the home of Mary and Joseph in Nazareth.

Any person who does settle to live in a bed sitter for life for those reasons will need a great deal of courage and a lot of inner stability, because a bed sitter in someone else's house is not somewhere we can ever put down roots.

What about a rented flat or a rented house? That would be better—so long as the rent wasn't too high.

But there is an appalling shortage of rented accommodation, and the rents are usually enormous, especially in the South of England. That is why people on low incomes, such as nurses, are having to moonlight and do an extra job on top of their ordinary one. It is why young teachers find accommodation such a problem. And it is why people from the North of England, who would like to come south for the jobs that are here, cannot afford to move.

My own opinion is that it is best to buy something if it is at all possible. Single women who have done so say that it feels so different to be living in a place that is really theirs. Occasionally parents can help with a down payment on the mortgage. Sometimes our salary is enough to pay the whole mortgage ourselves on a property. But the only other ways forward are either to join a housing association, to form a housing co-operative, or for two or three friends to buy a house together.

If I was in the situation of having to buy a house with one or two other people I have to confess that I would only be able to do that with people who were willing to live quite separately. I know that it would be necessary to share the bathroom and the kitchen, and I would want us to come to a prior agreement about keeping them clean and tidy. Other people's dirt and untidiness is something that I have quite a different attitude towards than I have to mine—especially if they are untidy in space that I see in any sense as *my* space. I see my own untidiness and spidery, cobwebby corners as having a certain artistic, creative disorder: 'Your kitchen is very paintable,' said one friend, gazing at the shapely clutter heaped elegantly over all my working surfaces, and when I had discovered he didn't mean I ought to emulsion the walls I felt rather pleased.

His flat is rather tidy, and he can always find things in it. And if I was sharing a flat or a house with anybody else I would want it to be tidy in the places we had in common. This double standard may not be an admirable quality in me, but at least I am aware of it, and I know that keeping common space clean and tidy in shared accommodation is one of the chief causes of disagreement and not getting on.

If I bought a house with other people I would prefer to have my own rooms and for my co-owners to have theirs. Ideally I would like to have a bedroom and a sitting room of my own, but if it wasn't possible to have two rooms then I would certainly like one, which I would use for living in and for sleeping in.

I know that there are some people who are perfectly happy to live together like a family, and if they can manage it then that is very good. But even in that situation I think everyone needs to have a room of their own into which no one else may go without an invitation. I rather approve of the houses that young people some-times set up in which there are both sexes, who live together like brothers and sisters, and if in my old age I have to buy a part-share in a big house I shall try to make sure that there are men there as well as women.

The lovely thing about having a place of our own, however small it is, is that we can make it into a home. It needn't cost very much, but we can create a room that will open its arms to people (including us) to welcome them when they come in. It can be a haven and a place of peace.

My living room has got very dark green walls, and a big dark green sofa and chairs that are getting a bit worn out from people sitting in them. There is a fireplace that has a log fire in it in the winter and an enormous arrangement of cow-parsley in the summer. On either side of the fireplace there are shelves with things on them: pottery wine chalices, green and white swans, little jars and white jugs and shining glass on one side (none of them valuable: I have mostly bought them in markets) and my grandmother's china tea service and plated silver teapot, jug and sugar bowl on the other. There are brass candlesticks and pottery candlesticks all over the place, because I love candlelight.

People seem to like to come into the room. They say they find it comfortable and relaxing, and I love to have them there. Whenever I get home my room seems to cherish me, and I love it.

People have sometimes come into my house and said, 'This is a happy house,' and I believe it is. I believe that God gave it to me, and when I moved in I did what a Christian friend, who used to live next door, did to their house. As she worked in every room she asked God to bless it, and prayed that the Spirit of Christ would come in and dwell there. Purists might say that the Spirit can only dwell in human hearts and not in houses. But it says that Christ is 'the image of the invisible God, the first born of all creation; for in him all things were created, in heaven and on earth, visible and invisible, whether thrones or dominions or principalities or authorities—all things were created through him and for him. He is before all things, and in him all things hold together' (Col 1:15-17). So that means that all the things in my house, and my house itself, are 'in him' and holding together through him—so surely I can recognise his presence, and ask that I might know that indwelling in all things more fully?

As C S Lewis once wrote, 'God likes matter: He invented it.' And I believe that God likes my house, which is made of the matter that he created. (I warned you that we would be doing theology all through this book, even in the practical parts!)

Can I suggest that you make your home comfortable? I once went into a house that belonged to a rather austere Christian and it only had upright chairs in it. Splendid for sitting upright and meditating on (you are supposed to keep your back straight), but not a bit good for relaxing in. Remember that people of different shapes and sizes and ages will be sitting on your chairs. Some people don't like low chairs (because once they have sunk into them they cannot get out again unless someone pulls them) and some people don't like chairs without backs that are high enough to lean their heads against. I don't. In one house I know I cannot get comfortable unless I lie flat on the sofa and rest my head on an arm. This is all part of doing what Jesus said we were to do: 'Whatever you wish that men would do to you, do so to them' (Mt 7:12).

The most important thing you can do to make a room beautiful is to light it properly. You will never create a really relaxed atmosphere with an overhead light, even if you have the most comfortable sofa and chairs that have ever been made. Spotlights can be all right (gentle ones, not fierce ones). But table lamps in different places are essential. Candlelight can transform even an ugly room into something beautiful and mysterious.

Buy or borrow books about home-making. Edith Schaeffer's *Hidden Art*; *The Pauper's Homemaking Book* by Jocasta Innes; *Superwoman* and *More of Superwoman* by Shirley Conran (useful tips about places to buy things). Buy curtain materials and bed linen in sales. Discover your local market.

Go to your local MFI Showroom and use your imagination. It is the cheapest furniture in the country. They are continually having sales, and one way of getting an even better bargain is to buy the furniture they have had on display. But it is unlikely that you will be able to put it together yourself unless you are good at carpentry (and that is not a sexist remark; most men can't put it together either). So pay extra and buy it assembled or else find yourself an odd job carpenter.

Find out for yourself about colour. The colours in a room need to blend, and different colours do different things. If you are starting from scratch then go around and look at rooms in shops like Sanderson's or at restaurants. Or borrow magazines, and get in touch with what you feel when you look at different colours and different decorations and ways of laying out rooms.

Look at nature. Put the colours together that God has put together. My room is the dark green of a cedar tree, the pale, clear blue of a summer sky, and the pink of an Albertine rose. God has made a beautiful world for us to live in, and he has made us in his image and likeness—creative and loving. So when we make our home beautiful we are doing what God has done in his world.

But just as God has made a beautiful world for us to enjoy, so we make our home beautiful—and welcoming—for other people to enjoy as well as us. We can entertain people, and the size of our home doesn't matter at all. One of the people I used to love being entertained by was a single woman who had just one room that was hers. She was the house mother at a Rectory, and because of the sort of person she was a stream of visitors used to pass through her room. She listened to us and loved us and prayed for us, and depending on what time of the day or night we went to see her we drank tea or coffee.

But we drank our tea and coffee out of beautiful cups and ate biscuits off beautiful plates. The tea was Sainsbury's China and Darjeeling, and unless we wanted it black the coffee in the visitor's cup always had the cream from the top of the milk poured into it. The biscuits came out of a small, round tin covered with blue cretonne, and when she asked me which of her possessions I would like to be given to me when she died I requested the tin. It was a symbol of her, and I wanted to inherit it because of what it stood for—a one to one ministry and friendship that happened over tea and biscuits.

Entertaining well isn't about the elaborateness of the meal. It is about the quality of friendship, and once people have found that they will be drawn to it like bees to honeysuckle. Emerson said that 'If a man write a better book, preach a better sermon, or make a better mouse-trap than his neighbour, tho' he build his house in the woods, the world will make a beaten path to his door.'

There are various things in the New Testament about entertaining. Hebrews 13:1−2 says 'Continue to love each other like brothers, and remember always to welcome strangers, for by doing this, some people have entertained angels without knowing it.'

One of the qualifications for a 'presiding elder' (1 Tim 3:1−3) was that he should be hospitable.

In Luke's Gospel (14:12−14) Jesus tells the Pharisee whom he has gone to a meal with how he ought to plan his future dinner parties:

> When you give a dinner or a banquet, do not invite your friends or your brothers or your kinsmen or rich neighbours, lest they also invite you in return, and you be repaid. But when you give a feast, invite the poor, the maimed, the lame, the blind, and you will be blessed, because they cannot repay you. You will be repaid at the resurrection of the just.

That passage doesn't mean 'don't invite your friends, your family or your rich neighbours at all', it is a Hebrew idiom.

The Bible makes it very clear that God has a bias to the poor, which means that we are to have a special love for them. We are to 'choose' to entertain them. But it won't mean that we invite the poor, the maimed, the lame and the blind to one supper party and our friends to a different one.

A widow friend of mine used to hate going to a meal with one particular couple, because she felt she was being patronised. She felt (although she was wrong) that they had their closest friends to supper parties and invited the poor and needy ones to Sunday lunch! When Jesus had meals 'with publicans and sinners' they wouldn't have felt patronised. They would have felt loved.

As single women we need to take the initiative in the whole matter of entertaining. It may be that married people in the church have never invited us to a meal. Well, so much the worse for them. But that doesn't mean we can't offer the first invitation. We may only have one room, but we can still have people to simple meals in it.

We need to be aware of the value of entertaining, and of what it can do for other people as well as for us. There is something very special about having a meal with someone, or with several people. I think that the reason why the single woman sometimes doesn't entertain, and never asks married people to meals (even if she occasionally invites her single friends) is that she doesn't feel she has much to offer.

That is why I have been stressing the importance of discovering our own value, and of being fulfilled human beings. There is a lovely bit in John Powell's book *Why Am I Afraid To Tell You Who I Am?*[1] He is writing about communication and telling another person who we are (or, rather, *not* telling). But we can have just the same uncertainty and fear about the offer of ourself that we make when we ask someone to come for a meal in our house.

The Human Condition

Consider the following conversation:
Author: I am writing a booklet, to be called *Why Am I Afraid to Tell You Who I Am?*
Other: Do you want an answer to your question?
Author: That is the purpose of the booklet, to answer the question.
Other: But do you want my answer?
Author: Yes, of course I do.
Other: I am afraid to tell you who I am, because, if I tell you who I am, you may not like who I am, and it's all that I have.

John Powell goes on to say:

> This short excerpt was taken from an actual
> conversation, unrehearsed and from life as it really is. It
> reflects something of the imprisoning fears and self-
> doubt which cripple most of us and keep us from
> forward movement on the road to maturity, happiness,
> and true love.

Entertaining is a part of loving life and loving people.
It will also include loving ourselves and loving food.
That doesn't mean that we must become gourmets or
gluttons, although we need to attend to the fact that the
enemies of Jesus accused him of being 'a glutton and a
winebibber.' So he must have enjoyed his eating and
drinking, otherwise they wouldn't have been able to
exaggerate his enjoyment and make that particular
accusation.

People sometimes say to me, 'Do you bother to cook
when you're on your own?' and I reply (in a surprised
voice which I have to confess sometimes has a bit of an
edge to it): 'Yes, of course I do! Why wouldn't I?' The
answer to that is something like, 'I thought it might be
too much nuisance.' So then I say, 'No, it isn't a nuisance
at all. I like food and I like cooking—and I like looking
after me!'

In fact I am not 'on my own' all that often, because I
love having people in, and I often go out. But even on a
Sunday, if I am alone, I will cook myself a roast dinner.
It may be only a pork chop, but I shall have it with roast
potatoes that are crispy on the outside and dry in the
middle, apple sauce and stuffing, perhaps French beans
with butter and garlic, and delicious, rich gravy.

Probably most of you are skilled at entertaining, so
this chapter is really for people who are uncertain about
how to do it. Here are some hints for beginners about
how to set about it and what is needed.

- A relaxed atmosphere. That means simple food, so that you aren't feeling anxious about whether the souffle or the Yorkshire pudding is going to rise or decide to be a pancake instead.

- Gentle lighting, with perhaps some candles (but make sure they are safe).

- Comfortable seating. Cushions can help, or the pillows from the divan put in covers.

- Something to drink when your guests arrive (it will depend on your views whether it is chilled apple juice or sherry), and perhaps some peanuts to nibble at.

- A casserole with baked potatoes, or a pasta dish with hot bread (preferably garlic: you can buy it ready made in supermarkets), served in either case with a green salad. Make sure the casserole gravy is rich and properly thickened and not like colourless cabbage water. You could buy Marks and Spencer's *1,000 Recipe Cookbook* for £1.25.

- Designer water (eg Perrier or Highland Spring) or wine to drink (again it will depend on your views, but whatever it is make sure that the temperature is right).

- Fruit for dessert—and arrange it so that it looks its most beautiful, perhaps on leaves if there is a tree anywhere near you can pick some from.

- Coffee and chocolates.

- Do all the shopping and make the casserole or the pasta the day before.

- Have proper table napkins that match the colours of your room. You can make them cheaply from a metre of Laura Ashley material or gingham cut into nine and hemmed.

- Have some flowers.

- Try to have five minutes before your guests arrive to just sit down and pray: perhaps in silence, or use the Jesus prayer, or pray in tongues—whatever you find best. But the purpose of your prayer will be that God will bless the whole evening. I sometimes say, 'Lord,

I haven't got a husband to be the host and to help
me. So will you be those things for me? And please
be very present with us at this meal.'

● Say grace yourself. It is your household, so it is right
that you should give thanks and that you should ask
for a blessing.

● Let your guest or guests know that you are pleased to
see them.

● Serve the meal you have cooked with at least a bit of
a flourish, and whatever you do don't say, 'It's just a
casserole!'

When I was an MP's secretary I helped another secretary who was ill one day by going to work for her boss
at his house, and he gave me lunch. I cannot remember
what the main dish was, but I shall never forget the
French beans. 'I cooked these myself,' he said (carrying
them in as if they were the Christmas turkey), 'It's a
special recipe with red wine and garlic.' So I ate them
with extra relish, feeling very honoured to have been
given such important beans. I told his secretary about
them when she came back to work, and she grinned: 'It's
not that Greville's beans are all that special! It's just that
he gives them such a build-up!' And perhaps she was
right, but it taught me a lesson that I shall always
remember.

NOTES

1. John Powell *Why Am I Afraid to Tell You Who I Am?* (Collins,
London, 1975).

7

Travel: Our Transport and Our Holidays

Our transport, or getting around

One of the problems that faces us as single women is how to get around safely on our own, especially after dark. In some areas it is not safe to walk alone on our streets at night time. So what are we to do?

Unless we are opposed in principle to any sort of violence it is a good idea to learn self-defence—not in order to hang on to our handbag, but to defend ourselves. Classes in self-defence are held in adult education centres and leisure centres, and they are well worth going to.

For getting around in the daytime a bicycle or a moped can be useful. Either of them will get us from A to B more quickly than walking. But a combination of public transport and walking might be just as quick, and a half hour walk every day will be good for our health.

Bikes and mopeds have certain disadvantages. When it is raining we get wet—wetter than if we were walking, since we cannot cycle along under an umbrella. We can get ourselves the sort of oilskins that deep sea fishermen wear, but they take quite a long time to put on and it gets very hot underneath them.

The feeling of freedom when we free-wheel down a hill, with the wind blowing in our hair, is great fun—so long as nothing gets in our way. The trouble is that things often do get in the way, and another disadvantage to a bike or a moped is that they (which means us) are very vulnerable. In wet or snowy weather they skid, and also the other traffic is bigger than them. A man I know who cycles everywhere has been knocked off his bike three times in the last eighteen months, and it has always been the motorist's fault.

We might decide to get around by using a mixture of walking, public transport and taxis. It might feel extravagant to take a taxi, but even to take one frequently is probably far cheaper than running a car. They are safer than public transport at night, and a qualified taxi-driver is someone who has been checked out by the local council and has no criminal record. It is therefore safer to use a registered taxi than any other hire car, unless we happen to know someone living locally who drives people around.

Probably the best form of transport for us is a car, if we can possibly afford it. But before we get one we shall have to work out what it will cost. Here is a budget based on the RAC's schedule of estimated vehicle running costs. The depreciation is based on the average price of a popular model, based on doing 10,000 miles a year over an eight year life.

Standing charges

Road Tax	£1,000
Insurance	3,730
Depreciation	4,800
Interest on Capital	2,700
Sub to motoring organisation	450
	£12,680

(NB This figure does not include garaging and parking fees, for which the RAC put in a figure of £3,770)

Running costs

Petrol	£4,700
Oil	250
Tyres	500
Services	700
Repairs & replacements	3,350
	£9,500

So the total cost of a small car comes to £22,180 for eight years (I have rounded the RAC's figures up), which divided by 8 is approximately £2,770 per annum.

This is a very rough budget and you would have to do your own. It will depend on how much your car costs, how many miles it does to the gallon, and how many miles you intend to drive in it.

It is essential to belong to a motoring organisation, either the RAC, the AA or National Breakdown. After I had waited for two hours in the outer London area for the RAC to turn up a breakdown truck arrived from National Breakdown (the other motoring organisations will call them in if necessary) and the driver told me (but then perhaps he would!) that they are always quicker at getting to the scene because of the way they work. Their HQ rings up the nearest NB garage to the breakdown and their van or truck sets out to help. Other people have also recommended that organisation, but I have never got around to switching from the RAC—who are always very nice indeed, and enormously helpful when they eventually arrive.

If we do have a car then we must help it to keep fit. That means regular servicing and regular attention to tyre pressures, oil and water. Some of us might want to go on a course to learn about the car's inside, but even if we don't do that then it would be as well to discover the basic facts about what can go wrong. If the engine is over-heating the fan belt might be broken, which we shall only discover if we know where to look, and in an emergency it is possible to make a temporary fan belt with a pair of tights.

I have just bought two motoring books for £1.49 (75p each, but they are packaged together) from a B&Q DIY Supercentre: *Basic Car Maintenance* and *Car Care & Accessories*. I may never want to renew my car's brake shoes personally (which it tells me how to do on page 29), but I certainly need to improve my confidence in using battery jump leads (page 10). And the Fault Finder section is very useful indeed with advice and guidance when (as their section headers put it) 'Wipers won't work', 'Replacing faulty wipers', 'Engine overheats', 'Indicators and bulbs', 'Checking the fan belt' and 'Passing the MOT test'.

It is essential to know how to change a wheel if we get a puncture. I know, but I have never had to do it in an emergency. When I have had real life punctures I have no sooner put the little metal prop under the car and started to struggle with my spanner on the first nut than some nice kind man stops his car and gets out. 'A damsel in distress,' he says (or something like that)—and I have to confess that I don't tell him that I can manage all right and that in the matter of changing a tyre men and women are equal. (They aren't: some women can do it beautifully and some men can't do it at all!) I tell him that 'I *can* do it—but I'm not very good at it,' and I watch admiringly while *he* does it. And I am enormously grateful, because I can only change a tyre very slowly and by dint of a lot of struggling with the nuts and bolts. The automatic tightening they get at the garage means they are *very* hard to undo, and I plan to buy a really good wrench and keep it with my car tools.

Until a few weeks ago I would have stopped on a motorway to change the wheel if I got a puncture at night, and I would have been pleased and not worried if someone stopped to help. But since then the motorway murder of a woman who was pregnant has happened, so

I doubt if I would stop. I certainly wouldn't if I was on a deserted country road at night. If I had a car phone I would ring up the RAC, so long as I knew where I was and could tell them how to reach me. But since I haven't got a car phone (and am never likely to get one) and hardly ever know exactly where I am when driving through the country at night, what I would possibly do is to drive on very, very slowly. It is perfectly possible to drive on a totally flat tyre. It may ruin the wheel, but it is a way to get out of trouble in an emergency. In some parts of the country it might be all right to go to sleep till morning and then set out on foot to get help.

It is always wise to keep the car doors locked except on motorways (they need to be open in case you have an accident and have to be extricated from your car). Two or three people I know have had the experience of men trying to get into their car at traffic lights, and in one case the man succeeded. He made the man whose car it was drive him to a certain place, but then the car owner told him to get out and, surprisingly, he did. I would find that very frightening, and I always keep my doors locked.

It is sensible to put a handbag or briefcase down on the floor where it cannot be seen. In London at the moment people are breaking car windows at traffic lights and grabbing the bag on the front seat! Another trick is being played by a person in one car who deliberately keeps bumping into the car in front. If this happens do *not* get out and give the driver that is bumping you a piece of your mind! That is what they want you to do, and if you do you will have your handbag stolen and might be mugged. Instead, make sure your doors are locked, immediately start hooting an SOS, and drive to somewhere public, preferably to the nearest police station if you know where it is.

As a car owner I used to be fairly irritated by some of the single women in my church. They would assume (quite incorrectly) that I was delighted to give them lifts and then, outside their own home, they would hold on to me as a captive audience by endlessly telling me their troubles. Keeping the car engine running and revving it noisily totally failed to get through to them, and I would feel resentful at being trapped in that way. It hasn't happened for a long time, and now I would simply say quite firmly 'I have to get home now, and I cannot stop and talk.' I may decide that I am prepared to stay and listen for a little while, but it will be my decision and not theirs. The freedom of going the second mile is a real freedom, and quite different from being forced to go the first.

Our holidays

I find that one of the nice things about having a car is that I can fling all my clothes into the back and go off to see a friend for a few days. I can also include wellies and my word processor if I want to. Then when I arrive the car is available for us to go around in, and if I feel like walking in muddy country I have my wellies, and if I suddenly feel inclined to write I have my word processor.

However, in the past I have found the whole question of holidays quite painful and difficult. I used to live next door to a married couple with no children. Twice a year they would go on holiday and I would watch them packing their luggage into the boot. Then they would get into the car and I would stand at the gate and wave them off. When they got back two or three weeks later I would have done their shopping and have a meal ready for them. I was glad to see them again, even though while they were away I didn't particularly miss them.

But as I waved them goodbye and watched their car disappear down the road I always felt terribly desolate. My singleness was thrown into stark relief, and I just longed for a husband to go on holiday with. I would not in the least have wanted to go on holiday with *that* husband, of whom I was very fond but who would have driven me to distraction. But that wasn't the point. What I had in mind was an ideal husband (see chapter 2, for my specification!).

Since then I have discovered that holidays can have problems. The family holiday is said to be one of the most stressful events of the year, when people are thrown into each other's company all day long with none of their normal chores and activities to occupy their time. Getting ready for a holiday is stressful as well as going on one, and that applies to single people as much as couples or families. We have to tie up all our loose ends at work and make our preparations for the holiday at the same time: clothes, money, travel, and all the other things that have to be done. But at least a single woman only has to do it for herself. A married woman normally has to get her husband's clothes organised as well, unless he is a very unusual husband.

However, since this chapter is about single women who don't have husbands, what sort of holidays are the best for us to go on? For some single women it isn't a problem. They go sailing or hill-walking or pony-trekking, or whatever it is that they happen to like doing best.

Some of us like going abroad and some of us like staying at home and exploring this country. But are we to travel on our own or go with a friend? I had a disastrous holiday once with a Christian woman who was set on evangelising the hotel. She didn't achieve it, because she couldn't speak the language. I had only just become a Christian, but she had been one for years and was training for the mission field, so I felt less qualified to make decisions than she did about how we should conduct our day 'as Christians'.

She decreed that we should spend half an hour each day praying together. This meant that she prayed out loud for most of that time and left me with nothing to say. I was inexpert and nervous of praying out loud anyway, and found myself getting crosser and crosser as every subject that I might possibly have tackled was dealt with in her marathon prayer.

Then she decreed that we should do Bible studies on the beach. So we did. I felt resentful, because what I wanted to do on the beach was to lie in the sun and get brown in between going for swims. I liked to do my Bible study alone in my bedroom—but of course that wasn't possible because I had made the fatal mistake of agreeing to share a room.

The final straw came when she dragged me to a bullfight, which I deeply desired not to see. A bull ran in and looked around the ring, a bit bewildered. A man promptly stuck a small knife into it with the purpose of enraging it—and I promptly burst into tears, stood up in my seat, and pushed my way out. I cried all the way back to the hotel, and vowed that I would never go to another bullfight, and never, never go on holiday with that particular woman again. Nor have I.

If we are going on holiday with someone we need to make sure we can get on. Perhaps we could have them to stay for a weekend first, and see if our personalities are compatible. I know that one of the ways God trains our characters is through people who rub us up the wrong way, like tiny bits of rock in the sea who are smoothed into pebbles as the waves rub them against each other and fine down their rough edges. But holidays are for relaxation and renewal, not character training. So we should choose our companion carefully.

There is a lot to be said for going on holiday with a group of people. Years ago I used to love to go on the Christian house parties run by the church I went to. We had prayers over breakfast and a Bible study after supper, and we would spend the day on the beach sunbathing and swimming and reading and cooking sausages over a fire. We went for long walks along the

cliff, either on our own or with each other, and there were
blackberries and sea-spinach to pick, and gulls to watch
as they wheeled overhead and sheep to look at as they
grazed on the short grass of the headland. There were
carpets of blue scillas, and orchids, and the whole air was
filled with the intoxicating scent of gorse. There was a lot
of laughter and, best of all, there was Christian friendship.

Last year I went to a summer school in Rome that was
run by a Christian organisation. There were about sixty
of us, and a few of us had gone together. We had lectures
in the morning and went sightseeing in the afternoon.
We had an hour by ourselves in the Sistine Chapel, so we
could gaze at those incredible Michaelangelo paintings
without being pushed by the crowd. We went to Assisi on
a bus and saw the tiny church that St Francis built,
housed within another, enormous church. We ate pasta
and peaches and delicious ice cream, and we had interesting conversations.

Going on holiday, especially to the seaside or abroad,
is a comparatively recent thing for people to do. But the
word holiday comes from the holy days of the church
that go right back to the Old Testament. They were
religious festivals: days when people stopped their work,
went to synagogue or to church (though obviously not if
the church was being persecuted) to remember the particular thing that the holy day was about, and then often
met with one another for a feast or a celebration.

It is rather nice to build a Christian dimension into
our holidays, because that gives meaning to the 'holy'
part of the word. It might be that we decide to do
something like keeping a spiritual journal, or do a special
piece of Bible study, or make a particular thing a matter
for daily prayer. It is God who has built 'holidays' into
the scheme of things, because he has created us people
who need to relax and enjoy ourselves—and that will
include enjoying God. The first holiday of all was the

seventh day of the week, when the work of creation was done. It says that 'On the seventh day God finished his work which he had done, and he rested on the seventh day from all his work which he had done. So God blessed the seventh day and hallowed it, because on it God rested from all his work which he had done in creation' (Gen 2:2–3).

8

Pets

The best thing of all about having a pet is that we can love it and it will love us back. God created us to have a relationship with his other creatures, so when we have a dog or a cat or a horse or a hamster that we love we are being true to our nature as a human being.

God created all things out of his love, so we are to love all things and all creatures. They are just as much part of God's creation as we are. Rebecca West wrote that 'Fido and Rover are partaking of a mystery of which, further up on the table, Cezanne and Beethoven are participants also.'

The medical profession is telling us now that it is good for elderly people to have pets, especially if they live on their own. There is a living creature to love and cuddle and stroke, and as well as that being nice for the animal it is also nice for the human! But it isn't only elderly people who like pets. Nearly everyone does. You will have read what Ruth Etchells' dog and cats mean to her, and what she learns from them, and you will also have read how much Patsy Kettle's dog meant to her.

My own dog, Timothy, meant a great deal to me. He was a small, wheaten-coloured cairn, with a large personality and enormous enthusiasm for life and for me. When I opened my front door he would rush downstairs from my bed (on which he slept if I was out) and bark a welcome and want to be lifted up and made a fuss of. He would rush ahead of me on our walks with his tail held high, plunging into bushes and following the enticing smell of rabbit, or hopelessly trying to catch a squirrel when it had escaped him by running high up into a tree. But at regular intervals he would emerge from whatever thicket he was in to look back and make sure that I was following.

After my father died my dog was there as an immense comfort. But finally he got kidney failure, and after being ill for three days he died peacefully on my lap. He is buried at the end of my garden with some daffodils over his grave and I miss him.

I suppose that is one of the difficult things about having a pet. Their lifespan is shorter than ours. On the first Christmas Eve after my dog had died I sat down on my sofa to listen to the service of Nine Lessons and Carols from King's College, Cambridge. As always, 'Once in Royal David's City' caught at my heart, with the purity of a boy's voice telling the start of the Christmas story. Then the choir and the whole congregation joined in to sing about the glory of it all. After that the great Christmas Bidding Prayer began and got to its ending:

> Lastly let us remember before God all those who rejoice with us but on another shore and in a greater light, that multitude which no man can number, whose hope was in the Word made flesh, and with whom, in this Lord Jesus, we for ever more are one.[1]

But at that point I dissolved into bitter, heartbroken tears. What about Timothy? 'It's not *his* fault', I prayed through my sobs, 'It's not his fault his hope wasn't in the Word made flesh, and it's not his fault he isn't rejoicing with us but on another shore and in a greater light. And I wept and wept, desolate.

Finally I stopped crying. But I still wasn't comforted. That only happened as the years went by and I realised what the Bible said about the redemption of nature and also discovered what C S Lewis's view was about animals and their owners. He believes that an animal who belongs to a Christian family is an integral part of that family. The creature is somehow 'in them' as they are 'in Christ'.

So on the resurrection morning, when our mortal bodies put on immortality and we are raised incorruptible, along with us will be raised our beloved creatures. Someone said cynically once that 'Jesus will be knee-deep in hamsters'. But I believe that the creator of this incredible world, with all its amazing number of creatures, will not find the problem beyond his solving. And I find it impossible to believe that the God who created so many creatures will wipe them all out like chalk on a blackboard. It says that one day:

> The wolf shall dwell with the lamb,
>   and the leopard shall lie down with the kid,
>   and the calf and the lion and the fatling together,
>   and a little child shall lead them.
> The cow and the bear shall feed;
>   their young shall lie down together;
>   and the lion shall eat straw like the ox.
> The sucking child shall play over the hole of the asp,
>   and the weaned child shall put his hand on the
>   adder's den.
> They shall not hurt or destroy in all my holy mountain;
>   for the earth shall be full of the knowledge of the Lord
>   as the waters cover the sea (Is 11:6–9).

I think that will only happen in the 'new heavens and the new earth.' That is also when C S Lewis thinks it will happen, and in *The Last Battle* it isn't only human creatures who come through the Stable door into the presence of Aslan, although it is the human creatures who

-can put into words what is happening:

> [Tirian] looked round again and could hardly believe
> his eyes. There was the blue sky overhead, the grassy
> country spreading as far as he could see in every
> direction, and his new friends all round him, laughing.
>
> 'It seems, then,' said Tirian, smiling himself, 'that the
> Stable seen from within and the Stable seen from
> without are two different places.'
>
> 'Yes,' said the Lord Digory. 'Its inside is bigger than
> its outside.'
>
> 'Yes,' said Queen Lucy. 'In our world too, a Stable
> once had something inside it that was bigger than our
> whole world.' . . .
>
> Then there came . . . a rustling and a pattering and a
> sound of wings. It came nearer and nearer. Soon one
> could distinguish the scamper of little feet from the
> padding of big paws, and the clack-clack of light little
> hoofs from the thunder of great ones. And then one
> could see thousands of pairs of eyes gleaming. And at
> last, out of the shadow of the trees, racing up the hill for
> dear life, by thousands and by millions, came all kinds
> of creatures . . . and all these ran up to the doorway
> where Aslan stood.
>
> But as they came right up to Aslan one or other of
> two things happened to each of them. They all looked
> straight in his face. I don't think they had any choice
> about that. And when some looked, the expression of
> their faces changed terribly—it was fear and hatred . . .
> And all the creatures who looked at Aslan in that way
> swerved to their right, his left, and disappeared into his
> huge black shadow . . . But the others looked into the
> face of Aslan and loved him.[2]

Because of the way God made us it is not surprising
that two enormously successful advertising campaigns
are based on dogs: the Dulux old English sheepdog
helping us to decorate our homes and the Andrex puppy
tangling itself up with yards of our toilet tissue. The
advertising industry has made a point of finding out

what things attract us and pull at our heartstrings, because they do their business by getting in touch with the things we really need in order to sell us things that we don't really need.

We all need to relate to creatures in one way or another. So shall we have a pet or shan't we, and if we do what is it to be? An elderly woman I knew was very fond of her canary, and at least she didn't have to take it for walks. But I passionately disapprove of birds being caged. God made them to fly free, and when I see them caged I long to set them free. 'A Robin Redbreast in a Cage Puts all Heaven in a Rage' wrote William Blake, and it puts me in a rage as well.

For most of us the pets we shall have will be dogs or cats, or perhaps both. So shall we get small dogs or big ones? The small ones need less exercise and less food, and the cost of feeding an animal (and its vet's bills) is something that we have to take into account. When we are going to stay with friends and take our dog with us a West Highland terrier or a Pekinese might be more acceptable than an Alasatian or a Suzuki. Spaniels nearly always seem to get smelly as they get older.

A single woman I knew had a revoltingly smelly spaniel to which she was totally devoted. In the daytime it stretched itself comfortably out on whichever of her chairs or sofas it chose, so that all of them smelt of spaniel and were covered with hairs. At night she took it to bed with her and it actually slept in her bed.

Another single woman had a gorgeous silky-haired black bitch (no one quite knew what it was) which was endearingly friendly but not properly trained. It would suddenly decide that it needed some love and attention when she was in the middle of a conversation, and she would immediately break off and talk to it, sometimes in baby talk. That is a great danger! Our dogs and cats may be baby substitutes to some extent, but we had better make sure we keep the whole thing healthy and under control. If we don't it will be bad for the creature and bad for us, and not the way God intends it to be.

W H Auden wrote that 'A well-trained, well-treated sheep dog is more of a dog than a wild one, just as a stray, terrified by ill-usage, or a spoilt lap dog has had its 'dogginess' debased.'[3]

We ought not to get a dog and leave it alone all day. If we have a job that keeps us out of our home during the day then perhaps we could get two cats and either give them a cat door or an earth box. Two would be company for one another. A single friend of mine who had never had any pets before got two kittens which have just grown up into two cats. They play with each other and they play with her, and she says that she finds them a source of continual delight.

NOTES

1. The Bidding Prayer for Christmas from King's College, Cambridge: 'Lastly let us remember before God all those who rejoice with us but upon another shore and in a greater light, that multitude which no man can number, whose hope was in the Word made flesh, and with whom, in this Lord Jesus, we for ever more are one.' Quoted in *Parish Prayers* by Frank Colquhoun (Hodder & Stoughton, London, 1967).
2. C S Lewis *The Last Battle* (Bodley Head, London, 1956; Puffin (Penguin Books, London, 1964).
3. W H Auden *A Certain World: A Commonplace Book* (The Viking Press, London, 1970).

9

Singleness and Sex

Until we got hit by the horror of AIDS western society thought that on the whole it was all right for people to have sex with anyone they wanted. Now they are being a bit more cautious and saying that promiscuity is dangerous and that we must be sure to have 'safe sex'.

Varieties of condoms are prominently on sale in the chemists, and there are bizarre advertisements on television demonstrating how to use them. But casual sex is still seen as the norm, and couples 'shack up' with each other either before or instead of marriage. Fornication isn't regarded as wrong at all and adultery can be fun and add a nice bit of spice to life—and Christians do it too. A little girl I know went in to her mother's room and saw her in bed with the man she was living with. 'Mummy says that people sleep together when they love each other,' she reported. The mother, who professes to be a Christian, married her live-in lover after her divorce came through. But what has her daughter learned from it all?

The seeds that were sown in the permissive society of the sixties have grown up into twisted trees bearing a crop of poisoned fruit—a dark forest of destruction that desperately needs penetrating with the light of Christ. Paul says that we are to be without blemish in the midst of a crooked and perverse generation, among whom we shine as lights in the world, 'holding fast the word of life' (Phil 2:15–16). But often the church has gone to one extreme or the other. Either it has gone along with permissiveness in a feeble sort of tolerance or else it has been judgemental and disapproving.

Jesus didn't fall into either trap. When I was doing a clinical theology course several years ago the tutor took us through the account of the woman taken in adultery. His own view seemed to be that anyone could do whatever they liked, and he ended up this particular piece of teaching by saying triumphantly 'And Jesus said "Neither do I condemn you" '. At that point, to his considerable annoyance, I said, 'But that's not all Jesus said. He said, "Go your way and sin no more"' (Jn 8:11).

A long time ago I got rather involved with a married man who wasn't a Christian. The single Christian men I knew were not paying me any attention at all (nor to any other women either), but this man was attentive and delightful and attractive, and we were mildly in love. It was a very great temptation to have an affair with him, and a non-Christian friend kept urging me to go ahead. 'It'll do you both good,' she said, 'and you'll enjoy it. And his wife is so unattractive . . .'

But I somehow managed to resist, although it was very hard. It wasn't that I resisted because of the fear of what God might do to me for breaking a commandment. It was that I believed the commandments were all for our good, and that if I went ahead and had an affair three people would be damaged—the man, his wife, and me. I didn't want to harm them, because if I did how could I possibly be keeping the second great commandment that said I was to love my neighbour as myself? And I didn't want to harm myself.

I didn't think I could never be forgiven or restored. But I believed that deliberately to sin in that way would be to reduce my potential for ever. Not that God wouldn't or couldn't re-make me, and not that I wouldn't be totally happy in heaven and totally filled with God and the love of God. Simply that there would be less of me to fill. I would be a teacup full rather than a breakfast cup full.

I might have it wrong. But that was what I believed (and still believe), and apart from the grace of God it was that belief that kept me from sinning. Perhaps we shall never know what sin does to us, and it is a deeply complex issue and even the Apostle Paul had quite a wrestle with it.

> But what if our doing wrong serves to show up more clearly God's doing right? Can we say that God does wrong when he punishes us? (This would be the natural question to ask.) By no means! If God is not just, how can he judge the world?
>
> But what if my untruth serves God's glory by making his truth stand out more clearly? Why should I still be condemned as a sinner? Why not say, then, 'Let us do evil so that good may come'? Some people, indeed, have insulted me by accusing me of saying this very thing! They will be condemned, as they should be (Rom 3:5–8 TEV).

Once we have really settled for chastity and celibacy (unless we marry) then it gives us a real freedom for friendship with the opposite sex, even if they are married. But we need to be careful. Lunch with a man is one thing. Dinner by candlelight in a romantic restaurant is entirely another thing.

If we are working with men the same rules of carefulness and chastity still apply. It is dangerously easy to get too close emotionally if we are working closely together. If we have got absolute standards then we shall probably be all right. If we haven't we shall probably be in trouble. If a man says 'I like being with you,' that feels good. But it doesn't mean that if he is married he doesn't like being with his wife. The danger signal to recognise is when we find ourselves daydreaming about him, and unless we want to get hurt we had better be brisk with ourselves. And we are being very naive if we imagine that our own Christianity or his will mean that this problem will never arise.

But the whole question of sex and singleness is a hard one. Most of us would like the close and tender love and companionship of which making love is the natural expression. We want the happiness that two people know when they are really in love, and we want the joy of a deeply personal relationship in which we love and are loved in ever increasing measure. Most of us would love to be happily married.

Sometimes it hurts so much that we aren't that we cry our hearts out. Why has God given us this lonely path to walk, and why doesn't he produce the sort of husband we're longing for. When we are hurting like that the only thing we can do is to go to Christ and ask him to bear our heartache with us. He knows what it is like to be single, and he can comfort us. And we need to remind ourselves in the midst of our tears that God has a plan, and that he knows just what his particular purpose is for us. And it might help to remember that in heaven there will be no marriage or giving in marriage.

If we are in that sort of mood, and aching for the love and companionship of marriage, then we had better be careful what we watch on television. It is very common to see people take all their clothes off and get into bed with each other, and if we are feeling sexy ourselves it will be anything but helpful to look at them. What is then quite likely to happen is that we shall go to bed and imagine someone is making love to us—and we shall end up either very frustrated or masturbating. That may be a way of relief, but solitary sex isn't the way it's meant to be, so there is a sadness about it even in the midst of the relief.

Women are most likely to get into this sort of 'longing

for sex' mood at two particular times in the menstrual cycle. Around the middle, when the egg is ready for fertilization and before it drops, and then again just before a period is due to begin. An awareness of this physical factor doesn't make the longing any easier to put up with, but at least we know it won't go on at that level for long.

Perhaps it helps to realise that a person is not fulfilled because she has a satisfactory sex life but that quite the opposite is true. It is only a mature, fulfilled person who will be able to have a really satisfactory sex life. Promiscuous sex is a mark of deep-seated immaturity. Over-passivity or frigidity in the female, or a lack of virility in the male, are also marks of an immature, neurotic personality.

An individual who is psychologically incapable of 'giving' in the sense of giving herself or himself as a person, and knowing and being known in depth, may be able to perfect a technique of sex. But it will never symbolise the deep personal commitment which it is meant to be and in which the deepest satisfaction is to be found. People sometimes think that all they need for married bliss and sexual fulfilment is a copy of the Karma Sutra or another good sex manual. But to think that is to get it badly wrong.

The whole question of sexual relations is complex, and couples who are completely faithful to each other and who have children are not always mature. Immaturity, as well as being the chief cause of promiscuity, is also seen by many marriage guidance counsellors and psychiatrists as the most common cause of marriage breakdown and marital disharmony.

One mark of immaturity is an inability to give, and in *God is With Us* Ladislaus Boros says something which is very relevant to single sexuality and the way we can express ourselves.

The banner under which love comes to fulfilment reads:

'I make no claim.' Love renounces any possessiveness, and flees from every urge to enslave another. On the contrary, it makes an offer. And what love offers is not one thing or another but 'itself;' basically, love gives neither the body, nor talents, nor qualities, nor riches, nor any other 'possessions'; it gives the very essence of a person, his own self. In this act of pure giving it is the giver himself who becomes the gift. The other opens himself to receive the gift, gives himself in the same way, and this is an act of grace. For each one knows that he can never deserve this giving, in which the other gives him what is most his own. And this is the glorious and marvellous thing about love. The gift that is given in love is ultimately always the giver himself.[1]

As single women the way for us to express our sexuality is to develop into mature people who are able to love and give ourselves in love to other people. Jesus was the most loving person there has ever been, and the most fully human person who has ever lived. He was 'made perfect through suffering,' but he achieved his rich humanity without the satisfaction of his sexual desires. So the fact that we don't have sex doesn't mean that we lack something essential to our total fulfilment as human beings.

The world desperately needs to learn the virtue of chastity, and if we can show it to them as a lovely quality, and at the same time show how much we love them, we shall be letting the glory of God shine out in a unique way.

NOTES

1. Ladislaus Boros *God is With Us* (Burns & Oates, Tunbridge Wells, 1970).

10

Our Clothes and Our Appearance

On a walk one September morning I suddenly stopped
and looked at the old-man's-beard growing in the hedge
at the side of a field. It was at the point in its life just
before it bursts into the white fluff that gives it its name.
There were hundreds of silvery, spider-like seed heads
shining in the sunlight, and that was the garment God
had clothed them in on that particular autumn day. On
the next day they would wear a different garment, but it
would be just as beautiful.

Jesus told us to consider the lilies of the field when we
were thinking about our clothes. Even Solomon in all his
glory wasn't arrayed like one of these, so we aren't to be
anxious about what we are to wear. God knows we need
to wear something, and he will provide it. 'Seek first the
kingdom of God and all these things shall be yours as
well' (Lk 12:31) isn't some sort of trade-off arrangement.
It means that if we get our priorities right we will get
everything we need to do the job. But we won't find our
new clothes lying on the ground like manna if we go out
early in the morning to look for them. Any sensible
reader of the verse will realise that it means we needn't
worry, because we will have enough money to buy what
we need. But what are we to buy and how are we to
choose?

Perhaps it doesn't matter what we wear. Two unbleached calico boiler suits would do, one on and one in the wash. People might think us a bit odd but it wouldn't matter. The important thing would be that we were doing the vital work of seeking the kingdom. Yet the kingdom isn't just a private and personal thing within us, although it is within us. The goal to be achieved in the end is that all the kingdoms of the world are to become the kingdom of our God.

The kingdom is present when and wherever the will of God is done, and part of our seeking it is so to act in the world and so to tell people the good news that they can know the love of God and be forgiven.

We who are in the kingdom are like a city set on a hill that can't be hidden. There it is, sticking out for everyone to look at, with its inhabitants all clothed in calico boiler suits. A uniformed army fighting for the right. At first sight a person not in the kingdom might not be very drawn to it, though if she discovered that everyone in the city was very loving and joyful, with an obvious sense of inner peace about them, and if they rejoiced with her when she rejoiced and wept with her when she was feeling sad—and did all the other things that they're supposed to do—then she might not find the compulsory boiler suit too off-putting.

Yet she might take a wistful look at the lilies of the field and the trees of the field, and the immense variety of shapes and sizes and colours in creation, and feel that something didn't quite match up. If God had made such a beautiful world why did the people who said they were his sons and daughters look so dull?

Well, perhaps the boiler suits could be coloured? Not just unbleached calico beige ones. After all, God didn't make a beige world. He made the sky blue—and pink and grey and red. And he made the sea green and blue with white foam trimmings. And to look at a piece of dark grey granite under a microscope is to see a riot of

every colour under the sun in tiny crystals fitting the one
against the other. So yes, perhaps we could have coloured boiler suits.

But we would have to be careful what colours. Blue
would be all right. Like the Sloane Rangers in their navy
blue and most of the rest of the world in their blue jeans.
But scarlet would be out and so would purple, because
those were the colours that the great harlot wore in the
Book of Revelation. But then so do cardinals and bishops
and Chaplains to the Queen. And the children of the
virtuous wife in the Book of Proverbs were all clothed in
scarlet. It isn't easy to decide what colours to wear, and I
know more than one Christian girl who has been rebuked
for wearing scarlet because it was 'un-Christian and
unsuitable.'

Can it be that God doesn't want everybody to look just
the same? If creation is the model then the will of God
must be something quite different from beige uniformity.
My family and friends described my time in a particular
Evangelical church as my 'drab years', and perhaps
clothes are the expression of a person's self just as the
glory of the lilies of the field is an expression of their
nature—but God chooses what the lilies wear and we
choose what we wear.

Sometimes we wear what other people want us to wear
so as to please them. Wives sometimes dress to please
their husbands, and there is a continual debate as to
whether women dress to please themselves or to please
men.

At the start of life our clothes are chosen for us. But
there is a clash of wills early on. William, my three year
old neighbour, insisted on going to a party in his new
dungarees instead of the elegant navy-blue outfit which
his mother wanted him to wear. I went to my first dance
humiliated and embarrassed in laced up shoes just like
my headmistresses's, since my mother had said that the
high heeled pink ones that I had chosen were impossible

for two reasons—first they were bad for my feet and second they were 'tarty'.

Later on, my father banned calf-length skirts and boots because he said he wasn't going to have me 'looking like a Russian tart' (although I don't think he had ever seen one). It seemed to me that the group of people who my parents didn't want me to look like had latched on to an important truth, that whatever we wear makes a statement about who we are—whoever we are and whatever we wear.

The lilies of the field have no self awareness, but their clothes (for which they have neither toiled nor spun) tell us what they are: a dandelion, a daisy or whatever. But as human beings we all have some degree of self-awareness, and the clothes that we choose will say something about us to everyone who looks at us.

When we clothe ourselves we could be said to be sharing in the work of creation, and just as an artist has limitations so have we. Social customs limit us, so our creativity must flower within those limits. If we go beyond the limit people will stare at us and think we are outrageous or frumpy. Outrageous dressing gets more stares because it is usually making a sexual statement.

The fashion industry says what the well-dressed woman ought to wear and produces clothes in whatever shapes and colours the latest fashion happens to be. 'Pink isn't in this year,' says the shop assistant. But God hasn't abandoned it for roses and sunsets or decided that the trees shall wear blue leaves instead of green ones this spring.

Whatever anyone says to us about fashion (or anything else) we still have to look at it critically and radically to find out what it is really saying and what lies behind it. Otherwise we are letting the world around us squeeze us into its own mould, whether what we are being squeezed into is a Victorian lace-up corset or tight trousers. Modern clothing does tend to emphasise the

crutch, and what does this emphasis imply? Not a difficult question to answer! But when I wear these clothes
with their implied emphasis on sexuality, what am I
saying to the world and is it what God wants me to say? I
suppose it is *just* possible that it might be. After all, he
created the human body, and sex, and he might consider
our present attitude healthier than the church at its
worst. But on the other hand he might find it too blatant.
We had better be sure that we know what we are doing,
and why. And presumably God would have disapproved
of his female creatures squeezing themselves into corsets
which hour-glassed their figures into quite unnatural
shapes and also made breathing very difficult.

There aren't any easy answers to all this, but we still
have to ask the questions and find out the answers that
are right for us. But how much time should we spend
thinking about it?

'Wearing clothes properly seems to me to be a full-
time job, and as I happen to have a great many other,
more important or more amusing things to do, I cheer-
fully bag and sag and look as if I had slept in my suits.'[1]
That is what J B Priestley said about the matter. But he
had at least given some thought to it before deciding to
bag and sag, and in his photographs his old clothes seem
to be a perfect fit for the person he was.

What the fashion magazines used to recommend was
one good, well-cut garment. It will fit us, suit us, and it
will always be there to put on. We shan't have to waste
our time looking in our wardrobe and wondering what
on earth to wear. Probably with different tasks and func-
tions to perform we shall need more than one garment,
but we can limit the number.

But we still aren't quite there. How are we to choose
and what are the rules? I don't believe that there are any
in the sense of a set of external rules, because I believe
that the whole area of clothes (as well as every other area
in our life) is an interior matter relating to the heart. So

that the nearer I am to my true self, and the self I'm meant to be, then the more truly beautiful, and less noticeable, my outward clothing is going to be.

There is a lovely saying of Beau Brummell to the effect that if you notice how well-dressed a man is then he isn't. One definition of 'elegant' is that which is 'characterised by refinement, grace or propriety'—and true elegance is an internal quality.

'Today, elegance lies really within the nature of the person, rather than with what they could possibly wear . . . Today, someone can put on a T-shirt and be extremely elegant, because there's an elegance in that human being.' (Rudi Gernreich in *Supertalk*)

When the heart that has been healed and made whole does the choosing, then it quite simply knows that this is the right thing to buy—because the heart has wisdom and makes the right choices. The clothes then will manifest the person's true individuality. She is free to choose for herself and she chooses right.

Perhaps there is an analogy with the human voice. People who know about the voice say it is a manifestation of the person, and to release the voice (by learning to breathe, relax, articulate and make sounds freely) is to experience a release of the person. But voices come in different qualities, and even when the release is total and the expression perfect we aren't all going to be a Peggy Ashcroft or a Kiri Te Kiwana. But we shall be *ourselves*—set free from the things that constrained *our* voices, so that we can use those voices with perfect freedom. The words that we say will (as ever and as in all things) depend on who we are and how free we are within ourselves. 'For freedom Christ has set us free' (Gal 5:1) and the work of the Christ is to set at liberty those who are bound.

There is a false self that we are to deny and a true self that we are to affirm—and we are far less passive than the marble under the hands of Michaelangelo as he chiselled out his beloved David. We work out our own salvation and our own wholeness as God works within us 'to will and to do of his good pleasure'—and finally the person that each one of us has within him or her to be will be made manifest: 'clothed', according to Paul, and the final manifestation will be in heaven.

The Bible uses clothes and clothing as analogies and symbols. Adam and Eve become aware that they are naked and cover themselves with fig leaves. These don't do the job well enough, so God makes garments for them out of skins. There was a curious backlash from eating the forbidden fruit from the tree of knowledge, because to cover oneself up seems to be saying, 'I don't want you to know me, or to have knowledge about me, or to see me'—and perhaps clothing is both a cover-up and a revelation of how things really are. But Paul writes that one day we shall know even as we are known (1 Cor 13) and that must mean that we shall know both God and each other as at the moment we are known only by God.

When the prodigal returns home the father calls for the best robe to be brought out and put upon him. One day the redeemed will be clothed in wedding garments, robes of righteousness, and white robes, made so because they have been washed in the blood of the Lamb.

The church (or whoever Revelation 12:1 is talking about) is 'a woman clothed with the sun,' and the Christian warfare is waged clothed in 'the whole armour of light.' In a mixture of metaphors Paul speaks of the earthly tent that we live in being destroyed one day and of our then having a building from God, 'a house not made with hands, eternal in the heavens', and here 'we groan, and long to put on our heavenly dwelling, so that by putting it on we may not be found naked. (For while we are still in this tent we sigh with anxiety; not that we would be unclothed, but that we would be further clothed, so that what is mortal may be swallowed up by life' (2 Cor 5:1–4).

In 1 Corinthians 15 the clothing of mortality and corruptibility is to be put off, and the incorruptible clothing of immortality put on in its place. The clothing will precisely match the body. A seed of wheat grows into an ear of wheat, not an ear of barley. Every seed is given its own kind of body, or clothing, and each has its own particular glory, which is the shining out of its own particular nature. And so it will be with us, it says.

Perhaps it will be like the first Easter Sunday, and that to begin with we shan't know who someone is but that then, in a moment of recognition, we shall—and give a great shout of joy. And there will be an Easter Parade beyond all believing.

But our hope of heaven doesn't mean that we don't have to bother about what we do in this life—or about what clothes we wear here. 'Your will be done on earth as it is in heaven.' In heaven we shall be clothed with garments that are an absolutely perfect fit for our personalities and the people we are. So we can pray that what we wear here on earth will also be the right garments—and discover for ourselves what clothes we can wear to reveal our real self in this world to the glory of God.

NOTES

1. J B Priestley *All About Ourselves and other essays* (The author has been unable to trace the original publisher).

II

God's Work of Art

We are God's work of art, and something that always happens to a work of art is that people look at it and assess it. It will have an effect on them and it will also tell them something of the artist.

Last summer I sat on the floor of the Sistine Chapel gazing up at the ceiling and the murals, awed and entranced by the sheer genius of Michaelangelo. The beauty and skill of the paintings and the vastness of the design was stunning, and I thought of the months and years of exhausting, backbreaking labour that it cost one human being to make that glorious work of art.

Years ago, when I first read Oswald Chambers' *My Utmost for His Highest*, I prayed a prayer of my own:

> 'Lord, whatever it costs you,
> and whatever it costs me,
> may I be the most I can be for you.'

It wasn't that I saw myself as a high flyer among the saints. It was simply that I wanted the very ordinary person that I was (and am) to be the mostest she could be for God. Not a mighty oak tree, but a common black-berry bush that had the biggest crop of sweet juicy blackberries that it was possible for it to bear, so that the God who created it and all the living creatures who ate its fruit would be satisfied. And the blackberry bush itself would be satisfied, knowing that she was what she had been created to be.

But I knew there would be a price to pay and I suspected it would be a high one. In *Little Gidding* T S Eliot says how high.

> A condition of complete simplicity
> Costing not less than everything.

So far as God was concerned I was not thinking of the cost of my original redemption. I was thinking of the cost to him in terms of the energy he would have to expend and the persistence and patience that would be necessary to achieve my sanctification and salvation, or wholeness. So far as the cost to me was concerned, my prayer meant that I was willing for whatever suffering it would take to make me the most I could be for God.

I have gone on praying that prayer over the years. Even when things have been at their worst and my heart has felt it was broken I have somehow been given the strength to pray it through my tears, and I would remember what C S Lewis said about a broken heart:

> To love at all is to be vulnerable. Love anything, and your heart will certainly be wrung and possibly be broken. If you want to make sure of keeping it intact, you must give your heart to no one, not even to an animal. Wrap it carefully round with hobbies and little luxuries; avoid all entanglements; lock it up safe in the casket or coffin of your selfishness. But in that casket— safe, dark, motionless, airless—it will change. It will not be broken; it will become unbreakable, impenetrable, irredeemable . . .
>
> We shall draw nearer to God, not by trying to avoid the sufferings inherent in all loves, but by accepting them and offering them to Him; throwing away all defensive armour. If our hearts need to be broken, and if He chooses this as the way in which they should break, so be it.[1]

But God can take a broken heart and mend it. That promise is right at the heart of the gospel, and it was the work of the Suffering Servant of God to make it come true.

> The Spirit of the Lord God is upon me,
> because the Lord has anointed me
> to bring good tidings to the afflicted;
> he has sent me to bind up the brokenhearted,
> to proclaim liberty to the captives,
> and the opening of the prison to those who are bound
> (Is 61:1).

When I was feeling very sad once I heard Dr Leith Samuel preach on Isaiah 42:1–4, where it says that the servant of God 'will not break a bruised reed,' and he told us to imagine that the reed was a musical pipe which had got damaged. Either somebody had been careless and dropped it, or somehow it had recklessly got itself to the edge of its shelf and fallen off. But it didn't make any difference whether it was somebody else's fault or its own fault, because the heart of the story was about what the servant of God did with it. What he *didn't* do was to pick up the damaged reed and break it in two and then throw it away. Instead he took it into his hands and bound it up and mended it. Then he put it to his mouth and blew through it, and the sound that he played on it now was sweeter and truer than it had been before.

When we can see by faith the suffering and heartache of our single state are the things that God uses to perfect his work of art, then we can make sense of the pain and put up with it.

> We know that in everything God works for good with those who love him, who are called according to his purpose. For those whom he foreknew he also predestined to be conformed to the image of his Son (Rom 8:28,29).

Amy Carmichael told a story of how one day in India

she watched a silversmith at work in the bazaar. As he
heated the ore over a fire the dross rose to the surface and
he took it off. Then Amy Carmichael asked him a question. 'How do you know when it is pure enough?' The
answer he gave her was 'When I can see my face in it.'
That is the purpose of all God's work in us. To make us
like Christ.

> We are already God's children, but what we shall be in
> the future has not yet been revealed. We are well aware
> that when he appears we shall be like him, because we
> shall see him as he really is. Whoever treasures this
> hope of him purifies himself, to be as pure as he is (1 Jn
> 3:2–3 NJB).

So as the silversmith puts the heat on in order to skim off
our dross and purify us we can do more than just remain
passive in our suffering. We can help in the process, by
the sort of praying that asks to be shown what needs to
be purified. Like David's great penitential psalm after his
adultery with Bathsheba and his murder of her husband
Uriah:

> Behold, thou desirest truth in the inward being;
> therefore teach me wisdom in my secret heart.
> Purge me with hyssop, and I shall be clean;
> wash me, and I shall be whiter than snow (Ps 51:6–7).

To pray like this might be to take seriously the penitential seasons of the Church, Advent and Lent, and use
them as a time of self-examination—asking God to
search us and know us, so that the light of Christ shines
into all our dark places. The process will almost certainly
be painful, but after the pain there will be joy and
freedom.

Once, when I was making jam, I was too lazy to take
the scum off the top, and I put it into jars as it was. But it
spoilt the clear shining colour of the plum jam in its pots,

so I boiled the whole lot up again and took off the impurities in the scum.

In all these things we can trust and be hopeful, in a gloriously confident belief that for those who love God all things work together for good and not for harm. In the best book on prayer I have ever read, *Jesus—Man of Prayer*, by Sister Margaret Magdalen[2] (who is, please note, a single woman) she quotes a poem by Susan Lenkes:

> Stoop-shouldered,
> foot-dragging
> sighing
> resignation
> is
> not
> trust.
> Real trust
> bounces on eager toes of
> anticipation—
> laughs with the
> pure delight of
> knowing
> in whom
> it believes . . .

When we can trust with that sort of pure delight (even if we can only do it for some of the time) then the 'work of art' is progressing. If we could ask the Artist how his work was getting on then the answer might be something like 'It's going well, and I can see the likeness . . .'

But as I said in Chapter 1, to get the work of art right we have to work at it as well as God. Most of this book has been about how we are to work at it. Our work isn't just the job that we do. Our work in this sense is everything that we do—the whole task of living our life and learning how to love. We have been 'destined and appointed to live for the praise of his glory' (Eph 1:12), and to do that we shall have to exert ourselves and discipline ourselves. In the days when I went to All Souls', Langham Place, John Stott used to talk about 'daily, dogged discipline', and I thought he was rather depressing. But I know now he was right, and there is no way of growing spiritually without it—although it never excludes the trust and anticipation that 'laughs with the pure delight of knowing in whom it believes.'

One of the books that Christopher Bryant told me to read, shortly before he died, was *The Road Less Travelled, A New Psychology of Love, Traditional Values and Spiritual Growth*, by M Scott Peck, and in the second section he writes of the importance of discipline in our spiritual growth:

> Discipline, it has been suggested, is the means of human spiritual evolution. This section will examine what lies at the back of discipline—what provides the motive, the energy for discipline. This force I believe to be love. I am very conscious of the fact that in attempting to examine love we will be beginning to toy with mystery. In a very real sense we will be attempting to examine the unexaminable and to know the unknowable. Love is too large, too deep ever to be truly understood or measured or limited within the framework of words . . .
>
> One result of the mysterious nature of love is that no one has ever, to my knowledge, arrived at a truly satisfactory definition of love . . . I am presuming, however, to give a single definition of love, again with the awareness that it is likely to be in some way or ways inadequate. I define love thus:
>
> The will to extend one's self for the purpose of nurturing one's own or another's spiritual growth.[3]

When we spend time being concerned about our own spiritual growth and discovering what will help us to grow we are not being selfish or indulging in spiritual luxuries. The only way to learn the art of being a single woman is to find how we can grow into the human being that God means us to be, and then to go ahead and develop.

Some women spend hours every week getting themselves physically fit by jogging and going to leisure centres for classes. But the Apostle Paul saw far more deeply into things!

> Keep yourself in training for a godly life. Physical exercise has some value, but spiritual exercise is valuable in every way, because it promises life both for the present and the future. This is a true saying, to be completely accepted and believed. We struggle and work hard because we have placed our hope in the living God, who is the Saviour of all and especially of those who believe (1 Tim 4:7–10 TEV).

Two married friends of mine were rather overweight and looked decidedly middle aged. Two years ago they both went to the local health club and went on diets, and I saw them for the first time after that at a Christmas party. Both of them looked marvellous, and I told them so. They looked years younger and had taken off pounds in weight. Before, they had looked pudgy and unhealthy. Now they were physically fit, and had clear eyes and clear skins. I was enormously impressed, and decided to join the health club and improve my own physical fitness.

But spiritual fitness matters infinitely more. When people look at us, God's work of art, it would be lovely if they wondered why we were so happy and blessed and fulfilled. It would tell them a great deal about the Artist who worked on us.

NOTES

1. C S Lewis *The Four Loves* (Fontana, 1963).
2. Susan Lenkes. Cited in *Lenten Readings*, produced by St Michael's Church, Summertown, North Oxford, 1985.
3. M Scott Peck *The Road Less Travelled. A New Psychology of Love, Traditional Values and Spiritual Growth* (Hutchinson, 1978).

Making Friends
(and making them count)

by Em Griffin

'Making friends and making them count is more than the luck of the draw,' explains Em Griffin. 'Friendship is an art. This book surveys the state of the art.'

Friends stick with us when times are rough. They lift our spirits, listen to our complaints, keep us honest, make even mundane tasks enjoyable.

Em Griffin has spent his life making friends. He believes that most people downplay friendship, because they don't know how to handle intimacy. Yet in a world where we are conditioned to love things and use people, friendship should be an end in itself. By word and example, Jesus made it clear that friends *matter*.

Em Griffin shows the many ways in which we can attract people, how non-verbal signals can turn them away, why we can have strong opinions on those we barely know, and what it takes to make a friendship last.

A delightful book, studded with cartoons and anecdotes, for everyone who is a friend, or who wants to be one.

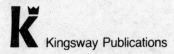

Kingsway Publications

The Final Boundary

by Adrian Plass

Life is a rich tapestry of emotions, memories and experience. Adrian Plass is one of the few Christian writers today who reflects that richness, wielding a pen at one moment like an artist's paintbrush, and at the next like a surgeon's knife.

To read these stories is to open yourself up to reality afresh. Whether you laugh or cry, you will perceive something new about yourself and about the God who knows us through and through . . . and loves us.

'Each story embodies a truth about being alive in this complex world that God created and has since redeemed through the death of his Son. They are truths that have been hard-learned lessons for me. You probably learned them a long time ago, but whether you did or you didn't I offer them with my love, and, above all, I do hope that you have a good read.'

Adrian Plass

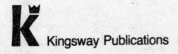

Kingsway Publications

Where Will I Find the Time?

by Sally McClung

'If I could just get myself organized . . .'

'I've got so much to do, I don't know where to begin . . .'

'I've found a system to work by, but I don't seem to have time for people any more . . .'

For most of us, the busier our lives become, the less fulfilled they seem to be. Sally McClung offers realistic advice for all those who want to learn to use time more effectively—for God, for family, for friends. Time to work and play. Most of all, time to live life in such a way that God can use us as he wants.

Sally McClung is married to Floyd and has two teenage children. Her active ministry within Youth With A Mission in Amsterdam is carried out within the context of a busy family life. Consequently Sally has learned to budget her time while still remaining flexible and open to the needs of those around her.

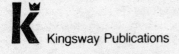

Kingsway Publications